西南政法大学公共管理学科 2013 年重庆市"三特行动计划"特色专业建设项目（行政管理）、2014 年中央财政支持地方高校发展专项资金项目（公共管理）、国家自然科学基金项目"专利维持机理及维持规律实证研究"（项目编号：71373221）研究成果

IP 知识产权专题研究书系

ZHANLÜEXING XINXINGCHANYE ZHUANLI

YUNYONG SHIZHENG YANJIU

战略性新兴产业专利运用实证研究

乔永忠　著

知识产权出版社

全国百佳图书出版单位

图书在版编目（CIP）数据

战略性新兴产业专利运用实证研究 / 乔永忠著. —北京：
知识产权出版社, 2015.12
　　ISBN 978-7-5130-4011-2

　　Ⅰ. ①战… Ⅱ. ①乔… Ⅲ. ①新兴产业—产业发展—
专利权法—研究—中国 Ⅳ. ①D923.404

　　中国版本图书馆CIP数据核字(2015)第310017号

责任编辑：刘　睿　刘　江　　　　　责任校对：董志英
文字编辑：刘　江　　　　　　　　　责任出版：刘译文

战略性新兴产业专利运用实证研究

乔永忠　著

出版发行：知识产权出版社有限责任公司	网　　址：http://www.ipph.cn
社　　址：北京市海淀区西外太平庄55号（邮编：100081）	天猫旗舰店：http://zscqcbs.tmall.com
责编电话：010 - 82000860 转 8344	责编邮箱：liujiang@cnipr.com
发行电话：010 - 82000860 转 8101/8102	发行传真：010 - 82000893/82005070/82000270
印　　刷：保定市中画美凯印刷有限公司	经　　销：各大网上书店、新华书店及相关专业书店
开　　本：880 mm × 1230 mm 1/32	印　　张：8
版　　次：2015 年 12 月第一版	印　　次：2015 年 12 月第一次印刷
字　　数：178 千字	定　　价：26.00元

ISBN 978-7-5130-4011-2

前　言

重大经济危机通常会孕育和催生一批新兴产业，成为新的经济增长点和摆脱经济危机的重要动力。在全球新兴产业知识产权发展新趋势背景下，为了更好地发展我国战略性新兴产业，国务院相关部门和最高人民法院发布指导战略性新兴产业发展的相关文件。国务院办公厅转发国家知识产权局等十部门联合制定的《关于加强战略性新兴产业知识产权工作的若干意见》指出，战略性新兴产业创新要素密集，投资风险大，发展国际化，国际竞争激烈，对知识产权创造和运用依赖强，对知识产权管理和保护要求高。做好战略性新兴产业知识产权工作，关系培育战略性新兴产业的成效和战略性新兴产业未来发展。最高人民法院发布的《关于充分发挥知识产权审判职能作用，推动社会主义文化大发展大繁荣和促进经济自主协调发展若干问题的意见》指出，要准确贯彻专利法立法精神和正确进行侵权判定，加强对战略性新兴产业知识产权保护，推动技术突破和技术创新，加快培育和发展战略性新兴产业。国家知识产权局局长申长雨认为，专利支撑经济社会发展要做好专利的产业布局，尤其是围绕我国传统优势产业和战略性新兴产业做好专利布局，促进产业转型升级，加快实现从全球产业链低端向高端的转移。国家知识产权局原局长田力普认为，新兴产业领域知识产权呈现新的发展趋势，即战略性新兴产业领域的专利申请量和授权量迅速增加；战略性新兴产业企业高度重视专利布局；专业化和有明确市场目的的专利组合大量出现；企业围绕知识产权的竞争与合作形式更加复杂。可见，专利制度能够有效促进战略性新兴产业发展已经成为共识。在此背景下，研究专利制度促进战略性新兴产业发展机理以及通过相关企业的数据对我国战略性新兴产业的专利布局和专利运用等问题进行实证研究，对发展我国战略性新兴产业具有一定的理论价值和现实意义。

本书在国家知识产权局软科学项目"专利制度促进我国战略性新兴产业发展研究——以全球新兴产业知识产权竞争新趋势为背景"（项目编号：SS13-A-09）研究成果基础上完成。本书出版得到西南政法大学公共管理学科2013年重庆市"三特行动计划"特色专业建设项目（行政管理），2014年中央财政支持地方高校发展专项资金项目（公共管理）的资助支持以及国家自然科学基金项目"专利维持机理及维持规律实证研究"（项目编号：71373221）的资助。本书第四部分至第六部分分别由乔永忠和梁齐、乔永忠和张恬恬、乔永忠和刘思汶合作完成，其余部分由乔永忠独立完成。

　　由于作者学识时间所限，本书难免存在不当之处，敬请各位专家、学者、同人等不吝赐教，提出批评指正，以便完善和修订。

内容摘要

战略性新兴产业技术积累和产业化态势引发了知识产权竞争的新趋势。培育和发展战略性新兴产业，对调整和升级产业结构以及转变经济发展方式，提升创新主体技术创新水平和竞争能力，促进我国科技、经济和社会快速、健康和可持续发展具有重要的现实意义。本书主要针对这种新的知识产权国际发展趋势，从专利制度视角研究我国战略性新兴产业发展中存在的问题，并提出对策。主要内容结构如下。

（1）专利制度促进战略性新兴产业发展的作用机理。专利制度鼓励和推动技术的创新和进步，推进产业经济发展，已经成为共识。战略性新兴产业作为推动产业结构调整的重要力量，具有创新依赖性强、成长风险性大、国际竞争性强等特点。专利制度如何促进战略性新兴产业发展，是第一部分研究的重要内容。具体从以下两方面研究：一是战略性新兴产业的概念和特征；二是专利及专利制度对促进战略性新兴产业发展的关键作用和战略性新兴产业对专利制度实施的特别要求。

（2）基于专利相关制度的我国战略性新兴产业专利

数量和结构及其发展趋势及问题。近5年来，世界范围内战略性新兴产业领域的专利数量激增，发明专利申请量增速显著加快，是同期传统产业领域发明专利申请平均增速的3~4倍。第二部分主要在确定战略性新兴产业主要产业与专利国际分类号（IPC）对应的基础上，分析战略性新兴产业及其各产业授权发明专利变化趋势及国内外创新主体在我国授权发明专利趋势，战略性新兴产业国外创新主体在我国授权发明专利分布以及国内创新主体在我国授权发明专利地区分布等问题。

（3）我国战略性新兴产业领域专利数量、质量和结构情况关系到我国未来国际竞争中所处的位置。第三部分以我国战略性新兴产业中节能环保产业为例，分析其专利申请量、授权量及其增长速度，并从专利申请、审查程序、授权标准和维持制度层面深入分析其存在的问题。

（4）基于专利相关制度的我国战略性新兴产业的专利布局及问题。在发展战略性新兴产业过程中，首要任务是发掘具有引领带动作用并且能够实现突破的若干重点技术方向，所以在全球范围内战略性新兴产业中涌现出大量战略目标明确的专利组合的同时，所属企业均非常重视专利的科学布局。为此，第四部分主要选择战略性新兴产业中新能源汽车产业中四家代表性企业为例，深入分析其战略性新兴产业的专利布局情况及其存在的问题。

（5）基于专利相关制度的我国战略性新兴产业代表企业专利合作模式及问题。随着全球范围内战略性新兴产业的迅速发展，企业围绕专利的竞争与合作形式更加复杂。一方面，由于战略性新兴产业的发展依赖于共性关键技术的突破，以专利为纽带的创新合作更加多样，新型技术创新联盟和专利联盟不断涌现。另一方面，新技术突破和市场策略变化致使专利纠纷愈加频繁，专利诉讼成为影响市场竞争格局的重要手段。为此，第五部分以战略性新兴产业中新一代信息技术产业中四家代表性企业的专利许可状况为例，深入分析我国战略性新兴产业专利技术合作模式及其存在问题。

（6）运用专利制度促进我国战略性新兴产业发展的对策。专利在战略性新兴产业中的积极创造和有效运用会极大促进产业发展。只有加强专利保护和管理水平，才能确保战略性新兴产业的企业实现创新收益，实现创新要素的合理配置和创新资源的有效利用，从而促进我国战略性新兴产业健康、快速发展。为此，第六部分从专利制度中关键机制出发，以前四个方面研究为基础，结合我国实际，提出应对策略。

目　录

一、引 言

在全球新兴产业知识产权发展新趋势背景下，为了更好地发展我国战略性新兴产业，国务院相关部门和最高人民法院发布了指导战略性新兴产业发展的相关文件。2014年5月，国家发展改革委和国家信息中心共同召开的战略性新兴产业发展形势座谈会认为，创新已经成为战略性新兴产业能否实现快速发展的决定因素，呼吁加强对区域战略性新兴产业发展布局的统筹和引导。❶ 2012年4月28日，国务院办公厅转发国家知识产权局等十部门联合制定的《关于加强战略性新兴产业知识产权工作的若干意见》指出，战略性新兴产业创新要素密集，投资风险大，发展国际化，国际竞争激烈，对知识产权创造和运用依赖强，对知识产权管理和保护要求高。做好战略性新兴产业知识产权工作，关系培育战略性新兴

---

❶ 国家信息中心信息资源开发部战略性新兴产业研究小组："2014年一季度战略性新兴产业发展形势调研报告"，载http://www.sic.gov.cn/News/82/2719.htm，2014-05-31。

产业的成效和战略性新兴产业未来发展。❶ 最高人民法院发布的《关于充分发挥知识产权审判职能作用，推动社会主义文化大发展大繁荣和促进经济自主协调发展若干问题的意见》指出，要准确贯彻专利法立法精神和正确进行侵权判定，加强对战略性新兴产业知识产权保护，推动技术突破和技术创新，加快培育和发展战略性新兴产业。❷ 不难看出，中央政府相关部门及最高司法机构都出台相关知识产权政策促进我国战略性新兴产业发展。

2014年4月22日，国家知识产权局局长申长雨在"2013年中国知识产权发展状况"新闻发布会讲话认为，专利支撑经济社会发展要做好专利的产业布局，尤其是围绕我国传统优势产业和战略性新兴产业做好专利布局，促进产业转型升级，加快实现从全球产业链低端向高端的转移。2012年5月4日，国家知识产权局原局长田力普在《经济日报》发表的"知识产权是培育和发展战略性新兴产业的关键"中指出，新兴产业领域知识产

---

❶ 国家知识产权局、发展改革委、教育部、科技部、工业和信息化部、财政部、商务部、工商总局、版权局、中科院："关于加强战略性新兴产业知识产权工作的若干意见"，载http://www.gov.cn/zwgk/2012-05/02/content_2127881.htm，2014-06-11。

❷ 最高人民法院："关于充分发挥知识产权审判职能作用，推动社会主义文化大发展大繁荣和促进经济自主协调发展若干问题的意见"，载http://www.court.gov.cn/zscq/dcyj/201205/t20120509_176751.html，2014-06-11。

权已成为各国竞争的焦点，并出现如下四点新的发展趋势：（1）世界范围内战略性新兴产业领域的专利数量激增，发明专利申请量增速显著加快；（2）专利布局已经成为战略性新兴产业先发企业抢占制高点的首选策略，各国聚焦战略性新兴产业领域未来竞争的态势已然十分明显；（3）知识产权竞争已经演变为包括一定数量且有内在联系的知识产权集合竞争，专业化、有明确市场目的的专利创造和运营组合大量出现；（4）企业围绕知识产权的竞争与合作形式更加复杂。❶可见，国家知识产权局主要领导对专利制度促进经济发展给予高度重视。

其他有关领导和学者对战略性新兴产业知识产权工作也发表一系列重要观点和建议。如国家知识产权局原副局长李玉光认为，加快培育和发展战略性新兴产业是推进产业结构升级、加快经济发展方式转变的重大战略选择。然而，我国在战略性新兴产业领域的知识产权发展态势不容乐观：（1）发达国家格外重视在我国进行知识产权布局；（2）各主要技术领域的核心技术多为国外跨国公司把控；（3）我国战略性新兴产业领域专利申请以国内申请为主，企业缺乏国际布局和参与全球竞争

---

❶ 田力普："知识产权是培育和发展战略性新兴产业的关键"，载http://www.sipo.gov.cn/yw/2012/201205/t20120504_685675.html，2014-06-11。

的意识。❶ 国家知识产权局知识产权发展研究中心原主任毛金生认为，在培育战略性新兴产业过程中，要创造良好的知识产权保护和运用的制度环境、鼓励和推动核心技术的自主创新、加强知识产权预警、合理确定知识产权保护范围、出台相关反垄断规则。❷ 毛金生等还认为，我国发展战略性新兴产业的挑战和压力并存，要做好战略性新兴产业内技术路线的预测和专利分析工作，尝试对相关产业的专利申请采取特别审查措施，制定有产业针对性的知识产权政策，积极推动知识产权国际合作，推动战略性新兴产业发展。❸ 国家知识产权局保护协调司孟海燕处长指出，战略性新兴产业发展引发知识产权竞争具有战略性新兴产业领域专利数量激增，有明确战略性目标的专利集合大量涌现，市场主体围绕知识产权的竞争与合作形式更加复杂等新趋势的同时，提出建立战略性新兴产业知识产权工作机制，加大战略性新兴产业知识产权工作的政策指导，切实引导企业与行业加强知识产权管理，有效促进知识产权运用等措施。❹

---

❶ "全国政协委员、国家知识产权局副局长李玉光专访"，载《代办处通讯》第158期，http://www.sipo.gov.cn/zldbc/dbctx/201204/t20120411_668060.html，2014-06-11。

❷ 毛金生："掌握核心技术知识产权培育战略性新兴产业"，载《中国高新区》2010年第10期，第18～20页。

❸ 毛金生、程文婷："战略性新兴产业知识产权政策初探"，载《知识产权》2011年第9期，第63～69页。

❹ 孟海燕："实施知识产权战略是培育和发展战略性新兴产业的关键"，载《中国发明与专利》2011年第9期，第17～18页。

国家知识产权局专利局汪陆洋根据国家知识产权局初审及流程管理部组成调研组针对新材料企业的调查结果和相关案例，提出强化专利意识、加强专业队伍建设、完善知识产权管理制度、及时申请专利等应对策略。❶ 国家知识产权局专利复审委员会张鹏针对知识产权创造、运用、保护和管理，提出如下建议：针对战略性新兴产业核心技术的一些技术领域试行依请求加快审查制度；完善针对战略性新兴产业核心技术的强制许可制度，并强化战略性新兴产业核心技术标准化进程中的反垄断规制；探索国际审查结果共享以及深化海外市场拓展目的国法律制度研究；完善资助制度及风险预警制度。❷ 另外，《科技日报》以"战略性新兴产业知识产权研究等待破题"为题发表了工业和信息化部科技司副司长韩俊和中国半导体照明工程研发及产业联盟副秘书长阮军等关于"加强专利分析寻求战略性新兴产业技术突破口"等问题的观点。此外，学者余江和陈凯华认为，提升知识产权战略能力是推动战略性新兴产业发展的基本保障和有效途径。❸ 他们还通过代表性专利深入分析发现，

---

❶ 汪陆洋："重视知识产权战略夯实战略性新兴产业"，载《新材料产业》2011年第9期，第79～81页。

❷ 张鹏："战略性新兴产业发展的知识产权制度回应"，载《中国发明与专利》2011年第9期，第19～23页。

❸ 余江、陈凯华："中国战略性新兴产业的技术现状与挑战——基于专利文献计量的角度"，载《科学学研究》2012年第5期，第682～695页。

与在华跨国企业相比，中国本土企业在七大战略性新兴产业的技术发展绩效也逐渐改善，但在各产业的技术创新能力上目前存在较大差异。❶ 郭淑娟和常京萍认为，增强战略性新兴产业的融资能力是我国抢占战略性新兴产业发展制高点的关键。❷ 可见，从国家权威机构到相关机构高层管理者，从专利审查人员到普通学者，对专利制度促进战略性新兴产业发展的关键作用都深信不疑。因此，研究专利制度促进我国战略性新兴产业发展机理，并对我国战略性新兴产业相关企业专利布局以及专利运用情况进行较为深入研究对发展我国战略性新兴产业具有重要的理论价值和现实意义。

---

❶ 余江、陈凯华："提升知识产权战略能力，推动战略性新兴产业发展"，载《科技促进发展》2011年第3期，第48～51页。
❷ 郭淑娟、常京萍："战略性新兴产业知识产权质押融资模式运作及其政策配置"，载《中国科技论坛》2012年第1期，第120～125页。

二、专利制度促进战略性新兴产业发展的作用机理

重大经济危机通常会孕育和催生一批新兴产业，成为新的经济增长点和摆脱经济危机的重要动力。为此，世界各国对新兴产业的高度重视加速了新兴产业领域技术创新和产业升级的进程。新一代信息网络、移动通信、物联网、云计算、大型集成电路、电子元件和平板显示等新兴信息技术领域，已经成为全球信息产业新的经济增长点，这些技术正在并将继续改变人类的生产和生活方式。生物技术在功能基因组、蛋白质组、干细胞、生物芯片、动植物生物反应器等领域的应用已取得重大突破，这些技术突破将在医药、农业、能源等领域引发系列变革。风力发电、太阳能光伏发电、太阳能光热利用、生物质能源等产业快速发展，新能源汽车产业化稳步推进，这些与新能源相关的技术将在全球能源消费中占据举足轻重的地位。新材料产品更新换代快、生产经济性强、产品性价比优、制造过程绿色化等特征使得新材料产业呈现出专业化、复合化、精细化的发展势头，并将为新一轮科技革命和产业革命提供坚实的物

质基础。信息技术将进一步发挥基础和支撑性作用，生物、纳米、材料等尖端技术将更广泛地相互渗透、交叉、融合，由此产生若干新兴技术和新兴产业，引发新的技术变革和产业革命，从而引发新一轮科技和产业革命。❶ 专利制度如何对这些技术领域进行保驾护航，进一步激励技术创新，为战略性新兴产业健康、快速和可持续发展成为值得研究的重要问题。

（一）战略性新兴产业内涵和特征

战略性新兴产业是指以重大技术突破和重大发展需求为基础，对经济社会全局和长远发展具有重大引领带动作用，知识技术密集、物质资源消耗少、成长潜力大、综合效益好的产业。国内外学者或者官方文件对战略性新兴产业的内涵、范围、特征进行了相关论证或界定。

1.战略性新兴产业的概念

针对战略性新兴产业的概念，国外学者分别从"战略性产业"和"新兴产业"两个方面进行论述。首先，关于"战略性产业"的论述重点强调其与经济发展的关

---

❶ 王征："世界战略性新兴产业发展走势概述"，载《中国环保产业》2014年第10期，第25~29页。

系。最早提出"战略性产业"概念的是美国经济学家赫希曼（A.O. Hirschman），他将处于"投入-产出"关系中关联度最高的经济系统称为"战略部门"。随后克鲁格曼（Paul R. Krugman）提出了识别"战略性部门"的外部经济性标准。波特（Porter）认为，由于科技创新、新的需求出现、相对成本关系的改变，或是社会与经济上的其他改变，使得某项新产品或新服务具有成为新产业的机会，并得到市场开发而形成的新产业。❶蒂斯（1991）认为，战略性产业具有规模和范围经济、学习型经济和网络经济的特征，这些特征使它具有强大的竞争力。

其次，关于"新兴产业"的论述突出其与产业发展的成熟度的关系。布兰克（Blank，2008）认为，新兴产业是充满未知性的产业，通常由一个新的产品或创意所形成，处于发展的早期阶段，存在大量的不确定性，如对产品的需求、潜在的增长潜力及市场条件都不确定，而且没有原有的轨迹可循。切斯汀（Stefan Kesting，2010）认为，新兴产业是指那些完全新的或者由于行业环境的改变而使其经历显著新增长的产业。也有国外学者将新兴产业划分为四种：（1）使用"The Emerging Industries"

---

❶ Porter M. *Competitive Strategy Techniques for Analyzing Industries and Competitor*. New York: Free Press，1980, pp. 120~125.

概念，表示新兴的产业或正显现的产业，具体涉及电动车、Web交通数据、数字电视技术、电信产业、制造领域、生物能源及生物技术等相关产业；（2）使用"The New Industries"概念，表示新的产业，具体涉及硬软件、信息产业、电影产业、移动网络、医学等产业领域；（3）使用"The New and Emerging Industries"概念，表示新产业和新兴产业，具体涉及绿色产业、园艺产业、生物技术、信息技术、农业、生物能源与生物产品、化学领域、高技术及其产品等；（4）使用"The newly emerging Industries"概念，表示新出现的产业，具体涉及生物技术、计算机软件、轨道空间、缝纫机、收割机、自行车以及武器、绿色建筑、老年健康等产业。❶

与西方国家学者相比，我国学者和政府机构对"战略性产业"一词的使用率更高。芮明杰等把产业区分为两大类：战略性产业和一般性产业。❷ 温太璞强调战略性产业在技术、体制和管理方面的创新特性及外部经济效应。❸ 李耀新、赵玉林和张倩男分别提出"战略支柱

---

❶ 孙国民："战略性新兴产业概念界定：一个文献综述"，载《科学管理研究》2014年第2期，第43～47页。

❷ 芮明杰、赵春明："战略性产业与国有战略控股公司模式"，载《财经研究》1999年第9期，第35～39页。

❸ 温太璞："发达国家战略性产业政策和贸易政策的理论思考和启示"，载《商业研究》2001年第10期，第25～27页。

产业"和"战略性主导产业"的概念。❶❷ 吕政指出，我国产业政策的重点应该是对战略性产业进行扶持和保护，绝大多数重大专项具有极强的关联性和集成性，有利于促进相关战略性产业群的成长，形成具有竞争力的战略产品，具有潜在的巨大经济效益。❸

关于"战略性新兴产业"，国内学者对此概念主要有两种译法：一种是使用"The Strategic Emerging Industries"，另一种是使用"The Emerging Industries of Strategic Importance"。❹ 国内学者就其内涵和标准的相关界定较多，具有代表性的界定有以下几种观点。贺俊和吕铁认为，战略性新兴产业涉及"产业""新兴产业"和"战略性"。"产业"是指生产具有相互替代性的产品的企业群体。"新兴产业"是指处于产业生命周期中"初创期"的产业。新兴产业的初创期持续时间因行业而存在显著的差异，这种差异主要是由产业主导技术的成熟度决定的。其中主导技术是指某个新市场中出现的首个集成了大多数能够满足客户需求的技术特征的

---

❶ 李耀新等：《战略产业论》，黑龙江科技出版社1991年版，第5页。

❷ 赵玉林、张倩男："湖北省战略性主导产业的选择研究"，载《中南财经政法大学学报》2007年第2期，第30～35页。

❸ 吕政："产业政策的制订与战略性产业的选择"，载《北京行政学院学报》2004年第4期，第28～30页。

❹ 孙国民："警惕战略性新兴产业发展的误区"，载《中国经济问题》2013年第3期，第45～50页。

新产品或新工艺；成熟度是指原有技术被新技术创新改进或替代的可能性。"战略性"主要体现在产业主导技术的未来性和突破性以及产业所面向的现实和潜在的市场需求规模巨大。前者决定了主导技术的投资具有长期性和不确定性，后者决定了战略性新兴产业的发展绩效涉及一国发展的深层次经济利益。[1] 宋河发和万劲波等认为，战略性新兴产业是指基于新兴技术，科技含量高，出现时间短且发展速度快，具有良好市场前景，具有较大溢出作用，能带动一批产业兴起，对国民经济和社会发展具有战略支撑作用，最终成为主导产业和支柱产业的业态形式。[2] 林学军认为，战略性新兴产业是指对本国、本地区有重大、长远影响，能够带动本国、本地区经济发展的新兴产业。[3] 朱迎春和王新新等也分别从国家战略意图、产业结构升级、新兴科技和新兴产业深度融合等视角对战略性新兴产业进行了不同的界定。[4][5] 李文增和王金杰等认为，战略性新兴产业应该是

---

[1] 贺俊、吕铁："战略性新兴产业：从政策概念到理论问题"，载《财贸经济》2012年第5期，第106～113页。

[2] 宋河发、万劲波、任中保："我国战略性新兴产业内涵特征、产业选择与发展政策研究"，载《科技促进发展》2010年第9期，第7～13页。

[3] 林学军："战略性新兴产业的发展与形成模式研究"，载《中国软科学》2012年第2期，第26～32页。

[4] 朱迎春："政府在发展战略性新兴产业中的作用"，载《中国科技论坛》2011年第1期，第20～24页。

[5] 王新新："战略性新兴产业发展规律及发展对策分析研究"，载《科学管理研究》2011年第4期，第1～5页。

指在国民经济中具有战略地位，对经济社会发展和国家安全具有长远和重大影响的必须具有成为一个国家或者地区未来经济发展支柱产业可能性的行业。选择战略性新兴产业的科学依据最重要的有三条：（1）产品要有稳定并有发展前景的市场需求；（2）要有良好的经济技术效益；（3）要能够带动一批产业的兴起。❶ 姜大鹏、顾新认为，战略性新兴产业是指那些代表当今世界科学技术发展的前沿和方向，具有广大的市场前景、经济技术效益和产业带动效用，并且关系经济社会发展全局和国家安全的新兴产业。❷ 朱瑞博认为，战略性新兴产业是一个国家或地区实现未来经济持续增长的先导产业，对国民经济发展和产业结构转换具有决定性的促进、导向作用，具有广阔的市场前景和引导科技进步的能力，关系国家的经济命脉和产业安全。❸ 牛立超和祝尔娟认为，从广义上讲，战略性新兴产业是指那些利用先进科技成果建立起来的一系列对经济发展具有战略意义的产业。这些产业普遍采用先进的生产技术，是科技创新最为集中的生产领域。因为其创新性突出、劳动生产率较

---

❶ 李文增、王金杰等："对国内外发展战略性新兴产业的比较研究"，载《2010年度京津冀区域协作论坛论文集》，第313～318页。

❷ 姜大鹏、顾新："我国战略性新兴产业的现状分析"，载《科技进步与对策》2010年第17期，第65～70页。

❸ 朱瑞博："中国战略性新兴产业培育及其政策取向"，载《改革》2010年第3期，第19～28页。

高，正处于产业生命周期曲线中的成长期阶段；同时这些产业需求旺盛，其对经济增长的拉动作用十分明显。❶可见，关于战略性新兴产业的内涵，不同学者关注的重点存在一定差异，所以对其表述的角度存在一些不同。

本书认为，界定战略性新兴产业的内涵必须了解"战略""新兴""产业"这三个经济学术语的定义。"产业"一词在不同的经济发展时期和不同的理论学派有不同的定义，单纯就产业经济学领域而言专指从事同类属性经济活动的行业和部门。按照产业经济学的发展阶段分类法和关联方式分类法对产业的种类划分，可以找出新兴产业、先导产业、主导产业、支柱产业和战略产业。从字面意思看，战略性新兴产业就是战略产业和新兴产业的交叉重叠。因此本书认为，战略性新兴产业是指我国在改革开放新时期作出的新的科技战略部署，是当今世界科学技术发展的前沿和方向，是新兴科技和新兴产业的深度融合，具有科技性、长远性、导向性、全局性和动态性等产业特征，关系到我国经济产业结构的优化升级和经济发展方式转变，对国民经济和社会发展具有战略支撑作用，最终发展成为提升我国综合国力和促进社会进步的先导产业、主导产业和支柱产业的新

---

❶ 牛立超、祝尔娟："战略性新兴产业发展与主导产业变迁的关系"，载《发展研究》2011年第6期，第77～81页。

兴业态形式。

2. 战略性新兴产业的范围

根据《国务院关于加快培育和发展战略性新兴产业的决定》和《"十二五"国家战略性新兴产业发展规划》，目前我国将节能环保、新一代信息技术、生物产业、高端装备制造、新能源、新材料和新能源汽车作为国家战略性新兴产业的发展范围，并提出了重点发展方向和主要任务。具体包括以下内容。

（1）节能环保产业。节能环保产业主要以节能产品、环境检测和污染控制产业为代表，主要发展目标为：重点开发推广高效节能技术装备及产品，实现重点领域关键技术突破，带动能效整体水平的提高。加快资源循环利用关键共性技术研发和产业化示范，提高资源综合利用水平和再制造产业化水平；示范推广先进环保技术装备及产品，提升污染防治水平；推进市场化节能环保服务体系建设；加快建立以先进技术为支撑的废旧商品回收利用体系，积极推进煤炭清洁利用、海水综合利用。该产业要突破能源高效与梯次利用、污染物防治与安全处置、资源回收与循环利用等关键核心技术，发展高效节能、先进环保和资源循环利用的新装备和新产品，推行清洁生产和低碳技术，加快形成支柱产业。

（2）新一代信息技术产业。新一代信息技术产业以微软、微电子技术和互联网设备为重点，主要目标是加快建设宽带、泛在、融合、安全的信息网络基础设施，推动新一代移动通信、下一代互联网核心设备和智能终端的研发及产业化，加快推进三网融合，促进物联网、云计算的研发和示范应用；着力发展集成电路、新型显示、高端软件、高端服务器等核心基础产业；提升软件服务、网络增值服务等信息服务能力，加快重要基础设施智能化改造；大力发展数字虚拟等技术，促进文化创意产业发展。该产业要加快建设下一代信息网络，突破超高速光纤与无线通信、先进半导体和新型显示等新一代信息技术，增强国际竞争力。

（3）生物产业。生物产业主要以生物医药、生物制造、生物育种、生物农业为代表，主要发展目标为，大力发展用于重大疾病防治的生物技术药物、新型疫苗和诊断试剂、化学药物、现代中药等创新药物大品种，提升生物医药产业水平；加快先进医疗设备、医用材料等生物医学工程产品的研发和产业化，促进规模化发展；着力培育生物育种产业，积极推广绿色农用生物产品，促进生物农业加快发展；推进生物制造关键技术开发、示范与应用；加快海洋生物技术及产品的研发和产业化。该产业要面向人民健康、农业发展、资源环境保护等重大需求，强化生物资源利用等共性关键技术和工艺装备开发，加快构建现代生物产业体系。

（4）高端装备制造产业。高端装备制造产业以航空航天、海洋工程装备和高端智能装备为代表，主要目标为，重点发展以干支线飞机和通用飞机为主的航空装备，做大做强航空产业；积极推进空间基础设施建设，促进卫星及其应用产业发展；依托客运专线和城市轨道交通等重点工程建设，大力发展轨道交通装备；面向海洋资源开发，大力发展海洋工程装备；强化基础配套能力，积极发展以数字化、柔性化及系统集成技术为核心的智能制造装备。该产业要大力发展现代航空装备、卫星及应用产业，提升先进轨道交通装备发展水平，加快发展海洋工程装备，做大做强智能制造装备，促进制造业智能化、精密化、绿色化发展。

（5）新能源产业。新能源产业以太阳能、风能、生物质能、核能为代表，主要发展目标为，积极研发新一代核能技术和先进反应堆，发展核能产业；加快太阳能热利用技术推广应用，开拓多元化的太阳能光伏光热发电市场；提高风电技术装备水平，有序推进风电规模化发展，加快适应新能源发展的智能电网及运行体系建设；因地制宜开发利用生物质能；该产业要发展技术成熟的核电、风电、太阳能光伏和热利用、生物质发电、沼气等，积极推进可再生能源技术产业化。

（6）新材料产业。新材料产业以电子信息材料、纳米材料、先进复合材料、生物环境材料为代表，主要发展目标为，大力发展稀土功能材料、高性能膜材料、特种玻璃、功能陶瓷、半导体照明材料等新型功能材料；积极发展高品质特殊钢、新型合金材料、工程塑料等先进结构材料；提升碳纤维、芳纶、超高分子量聚乙烯纤维等高性能纤维及其复合材料发展水平；开展纳米、超导、智能等共性基础材料研究。该产业要大力发展新型功能材料、先进结构材料和复合材料，开展共性基础材料研究和产业化，建立认定和统计体系，引导材料工业结构调整。

（7）新能源汽车产业。新能源汽车产业以纯电动汽车、混合动力电动汽车、燃料电池汽车为代表，主要发展目标为，着力突破动力电池、驱动电机和电子控制领域关键核心技术，推进插电式混合动力汽车、纯电动汽车推广应用和产业化；开展燃料电池汽车相关前沿技术研发，大力推进高能效、低排放节能汽车发展。该产业要加快高性能动力电池、电机等关键零部件和材料核心技术研发及推广应用，形成产业化体系。

3.战略性新兴产业的特征

2009年11月3日，温家宝总理在北京科技界大会上的讲话中指出，选择战略性新兴产业要满足三条科学依据：（1）产品要有稳定并有发展前景的市场需求；（2）要有良好的经济技术效益；（3）要能带动一批产业的兴起。由此可见，战略性新兴产业战略性体现在发展空间大、带动作用强、经济效益好、对社会和经济发展影响作用大，同时其战略性还体现在战略性新兴产业对经济发展范式的巨大推动作用，加快产业升级换代和经济发展方式的转变，决定未来国家的科技竞争优势。关于战略性新兴产业的特征，国内外学者有不同的表述。克劳德（Claude，2003）认为，新兴产业应具有：（1）突破性的创新；（2）具备市场化的潜力；（3）该产业处于产业生命周期的早期；（4）具有高度的不确定性等特征。[1] 薛澜和林泽梁等认为，战略性新兴产业有两个特点：（1）体现国家主导战略意图。[2] 战略目标的选择需要综合考虑促进经济增长、克服社会问题和保障国家安全。（2）蕴含全新发展图景。它可能由科学技术的革命性突破所推动，也可能是新的发展需求拉动的结果。[3] 蒋文能和凌荣安等认为，战略性新兴产业具有以下八大特征：科技含量高、融合创新性、不确定性高、战略导向性、可持续发展性、基于公共性的外部性、演

---

[1] Claude G. Dynamic Competition and Development of New Competencies, Charlotte: Information Age Publishing，2003.

[2] 林学军："战略性新兴产业的发展与形成模式研究"，载《中国软科学》2012年第2期，第26～34页。

[3] 薛澜、林泽梁、梁正等："世界战略性新兴产业的发展趋势对我国的启示"，载《中国软科学》2013年第5期，第18～26页。

化成长性、辐射带动性。[1] 战略性新兴产业是我国在改革开放新时期作出的新的科技战略部署，是当今世界科学技术发展的前沿和方向，是新兴科技和新兴产业的深度融合，具有不确定性、战略性、政策导向性、外部性、创新性和复杂性等产业特征。

（1）战略性。战略性新兴产业是对我国经济和社会发展具有重大战略意义的新兴产业，是在社会和经济大转型背景下提出的科技战略部署。有学者认为，战略性新兴产业中的"战略性"具有两方面含义：①战略性新兴产业对国民经济运行具有非常重要的影响力，涉及国家根本竞争力、国家安全、国家战略目标的实现程度，对调整和升级产业结构，提高综合国力和国际竞争力具有显著的促进作用；②战略性新兴产业具有范围经济、规模经济、学习效应和网络外部性等特征，能产生巨大的溢出效应，为传统产业及其他相关行业的发展提供相应的基础设施。[2] 战略性是战略性新兴产业的首要特征。

（2）新兴性。根据产品生命周期以及产品创新、工艺创新和产业组织结构之间的关系，产业生命周期存在

---

[1] 蒋文能、凌荣安、秦强等："战略性新兴产业的内涵、机理及政府介入"，载《经济与社会发展》2013年第4期，第1～6页。

[2] 郑江淮："理解战略性新兴产业的发展：概念、可能的市场失灵与发展定位"，载《上海金融学院学报》2010年第4期，第5～10页。

流动、过渡和专业化三个。战略新兴产业中的"新兴"具有三方面含义：从时间角度看，"新兴产业"是刚刚兴起的产业，与传统产业相对；从技术角度看，"新兴产业"必然来源于技术革新，将产生新的产品；从市场成熟程度看，"新兴产业"目前的市场容量较小，存在较大的不确定性，产品设计没有定型，用以制造产品的机器设备专用性强。❶战略性新兴产业的发展有着其内在规律性，因为"新兴"一词的相对性，所以不同发展阶段的战略性新兴产业具有不同的特征。

（3）风险性。战略性新兴产业作为新兴产业必然面临较大的风险，主要体现在技术、市场、组织管理、财务和政策的风险。①技术风险。战略性新兴产业的关键是技术创新，而技术创新风险不可度量。由技术模仿者变成同行者，就必须面对技术创新的不确定性和研发投入的高风险。②市场风险。一项技术能否被推广，往往取决于市场需求。技术先进不一定是取胜的关键，技术的市场需求、产品化成本、消费者习惯以及市场规模等因素都可能影响战略性新兴产业的发展。③管理风险。管理不确定性主要表现在技术创新和产业化主体的不确定性；企业组织内部的不协调性。④财务和政策风险。

---

❶ 朱瑞博、刘芸："战略性新兴产业的培育及其自主创新"，载《重庆社会科学》2011年第2期，第45～53页。

大部分新兴产业在发展初期都会遇到融资困难、资金不足等问题。

（4）导向性。战略性新兴产业除具有一般新兴产业的特点之外，其发展还具有政策导向性特点。国家相关政策对战略性新兴产业的选择具有信号导向作用，代表政府未来重点扶持的行业，是引导资金投放、人才集聚、技术研发、政策制定的重要依据。因此，战略性新兴产业的选择对产业发展具有一定的导向性。

（5）创新性。技术创新是战略性新兴产业发展的核心，战略性新兴产业的发展必须随着技术创新的进步，尤其是拥有自主知识产权的技术创新的产业化进程不断发展。战略性新兴产业属于知识技术密集型产业，技术创新是产业发展的内在需求，对技术创新的研发投入以及现有技术创新能力决定了战略性新兴产业发展水平和未来走向。

（6）复杂性。战略性新兴产业面临技术的复杂性、产业化的复杂性和产业链的复杂性问题。技术的复杂性主要表现在技术研发的长期复杂性，难以预期的相关技术支持和配套问题。产业化的复杂性表现在战略性新兴产业通常因为技术跨越多个领域导致的产业化复杂化过程以及产业链和产业分工的不同，需要企业产业链上下游之间密切配合，但是在产业发展初期，其产业链的各个环节比较难以协调发展，制约产业发展速度，增加战略性新兴产业的技术产业化的复杂性。目前，战略性新兴产业处于发展的初期阶段，具有很强的不确定性。现阶段战略性新兴产业核心技术和主导设计还不够完善，其核心技术、产业化、市场需求等方面的不确定性以及从创新中获利的不确定性等因素可能使得战略性新兴产业的发展过程更加复杂化。

值得一提的是，不同地区根据当地产业发展优势和区域特征，在此基础上确定的本地区战略性新兴产业的范围与国家战略性新兴产业的范围存在一定的差异。

（二）专利制度对战略性新兴产业的作用机制

发展战略性新兴产业已成为后金融危机世界主要国家抢占新一轮经济和科技发展制高点的重大战略。面对国际金融危机背景下的竞争形势，各国纷纷加大对战略性新兴产业及相关科技创新的投入，加快对新兴技术、知识产权和有关产业发展的布局，力争借此抢占新一轮经济发展制高点。战略性新兴产业是知识产权的密集区域，离不开知识产权的支撑。

1. 战略性新兴产业与专利制度

专利与战略性新兴产业关系密切已经成为共识。战略性新兴产业由新兴科技与新兴产业深度融合而成，技术与知识非常密集，其发展须依靠专利的创造、运用、保护和管理。高强度的研发投入依赖创新成果的专利化来化解重大投资风险。专利在战略性新兴产业中的有效运用会极大促进产业发展。只有加强专利保护，才能确保企业实现创新收益，进而实现创新要素的合理配置和创新资源的有效利用。同时，国际化发展和全球化竞争也必然要求专利的前瞻性全球布局。

（1）战略性新兴产业领域专利出现新特征。战略性新兴产业的技术积累和产业化态势已经在全球范围内引起该领域专利出现以下新特征。①大量涌现战略目标明确的专利组合，专利结构性布局成为重点。在电子通信、新能源汽车等技术高度集成的产业领域，单项专利的竞争力明显降低，专利竞争演变为包括一定数量且有内在联系的专利集合竞争。所以专业化、战略目标明确的专利创造和运营组合越来越多，结构性布局成为战略性新兴产业专利的突出特点。跨国公司的"专利包"和专利组合许可频繁发生。②在企业专利竞争态势加剧的同时，专利合作模式显得更加迫切和复杂。近年来，企业间专利竞争与合作状况，对其生存和发展越发重要，甚至影响到一个产业的发展方向。一方面，由于战略性新兴产业的发展依赖于共性关键技术的突破，多方甚至多国共同完成创新的合作模式是实现共性关键技术突破的有效途径，以专利为纽带的创新合作更加多样，新型技术创新联盟和专利联盟不断涌现。另一方面，新技术突破和市场策略变化致使专利纠纷更加频繁，专利诉讼成为影响市场竞争格局的重要手段。伴随战略性新兴产业的培育和发展，专利竞争会更加复杂。❶ 这些新的特征将在新的经济发展环境下进一步促进战略性新兴产业健康发展。

（2）战略性新兴产业发展引发专利竞争新趋势。战略性新兴产业的技术积累和产业化发展引发的专利竞争新趋势主要表现在以下五个方面。①战略性新兴产业领域专利申请量和授权量急剧增加。为了在战略性新兴产业专利竞争中获得优势，不同国家或者地区在一些基础性、前沿性、关键性技术领域争取提前获得突破，并获得专利授权，抢占技术先机，取得垄断权。②涉及战略性新兴产业的战略性的组合专利申请大量涌现。在电信、清洁能源汽车、生物技术、新材料、智能网络技术领域，很多产品都包含大量专利。单一专利在这些技术领域构成产品的可能性已经很小，所以专利竞争已经变成一定数量、形成内在逻辑结构的专利组合，结构性的专利布局将成为战略性新兴产业专利发展的重要特征。③战略性新兴产业领域专利领域将出现更新的合作模式。战略性新兴产业的发展依赖于关键技术的开发与突

---

❶ 田力普："知识产权是培育和发展战略性新兴产业的关键"，载《经济日报》2012年5月4日。

破，不同领域的创新主体，甚至不同国家或地区的创新主体协同完成技术创新的开放式合作模式将是突破关键技术的主要模式。由此产生的以专利为纽带的创新合作将引发专利联盟等专利有机组合的新模式。④专利运用将成为战略性新兴产业的重要推手。战略性新兴产业创新要求高，但市场规模小；增长潜力大，但投入风险高；市场国际化，但竞争更激烈。在新兴技术突破和企业营销策略不断变化的背景下，企业专利纠纷不断出现，或许将成为常态。这将使战略性新兴产业相关企业高层对专利运用和运营更加重视。日本、美国、德国等发达国家已经都将专利的高效运用和运营作为发展战略性新兴产业的重要措施。因此，探索专利运用和运营的高效模式，切实发挥专利对战略性新兴产业发展的促进作用，将是战略性新兴产业发展的关键之举。⑤战略性新兴产业领域专利竞争将更加激烈和复杂。随着新兴市场国家的迅速发展，其通过发展战略性新兴产业发展调整产业结构、转变经济发展模式的发展模式越来越明显。发达国家既要侵占新兴国家的市场，又要与新兴国家在更高层次上竞争，只能通过抢先在关键技术及其专利加快布局等手段制约新兴国家的战略性新兴产业发展。因此，发达国家和新兴国家在战略性新兴产业中专利的竞争将更加激烈和复杂。❶ 可以预见，专利竞争的胜败可能在很大程度上影响战略性新兴产业的发展水平。

总之，在新的国际竞争环境下，战略性新兴产业拥有自主专利的产品和技术是获得市场竞争力的根本保障。建立以专利管理为基础的产业经营管理体系，是我国参与国际市场竞争的迫切要求。正如施乐公司许可部前主任丹尼尔（Joe Daniele）指出的："知识产权管理是研发到市场的直接连接。"❷ 实施国家专利战略，大力提升专利创造、运用、保护和管理能力，充分发挥专利在转变经济发展方式中的支撑引领作用，才能全力推动经济进入创新驱动、内生增长的可持续发展轨道，推动战略性新兴产业快速发展。

（3）专利制度对战略性新兴产业发展的新作用。专利制度对战略性新兴产业发展的重要作用主要表现在如下四个方面。①专利制度有助于整合战略性新兴产业技术资源。新兴技术往往是链式创新，不仅需要企业的应用创新，更需要科研院所和高等院校的原始创新。这种原始创新能够直接产生具有知识产权的创新成果，解

---

❶ 孟海燕："实施知识产权战略是培育和发展战略性新兴产业的关键"，载《中国发明与专利》2011年第9期，第17～18页。

❷ Edward Kahn, Patent Mining in a Changing World of Technology and Product Development, *Intellectual Assets Management*, July/ August,2003.

决因缺乏技术专利等知识产权给企业带来的产业发展问题。因此,战略性新兴产业相关企业特别需要研究团队的通力协作,借助专利优势形成利益分享格局,通过强化专利管理,整合和增加战略性新兴产业技术资源。②专利制度有助于激励战略性新兴产业自主创新。专利制度可以激励研发人员从事技术创新的积极性,促进新兴企业将更多资金投向新的技术研发,有效激励技术创新,造就更多的技术优势。拥有专利优势的战略性新兴产业相关企业可以利用技术产业化赢得高额利润,提升其在行业中的地位,及时改进技术进行二次创新。③专利制度有助于战略性新兴产业价值增值。专利制度增加了战略性新兴产业相关企业的重要无形资产。相关资料显示,美国具有代表性的500家上市公司,其无形资产,包括专利和商标等,占全部资产的比例大幅提升。④专利制度有助于引导战略性新兴产业通过自主创新获得竞争优势。专利制度不仅有利于技术标准的制定,规范市场竞争秩序,而且为新兴企业技术创新过程中可能出现的创新纠纷提供了解决途径。知识产权管理贯穿新兴产业发展的全过程,有助于引导企业通过创新活动获取竞争优势。❶ 战略性新兴产业的一系列特征使得专利

---

❶ 贾品荣:"培育和发展新兴产业需要知识产权战略",载《中国经济时报》2010年10月22日。

制度从不同的层面发挥特殊的作用。

2. 专利制度促进战略性新兴产业发展的功能

有效运用专利制度是提高开发和利用战略性新兴产业相关专利效率的重要途径之一。专利制度通过合理确定专利权人对知识及其他信息的权利，调整其在创造、运用知识和信息过程中产生的利益关系，通过激励技术创新，推动进步和经济社会发展。专利制度对战略性新兴产业发展的功能主要表现在以下六个方面。

（1）专利制度是战略性新兴产业健康发展的重要保障。因为专利制度在我国的历史不长，相当一部分企业专利意识不强，使我国企业遭遇大量跨国公司的国际专利诉讼，导致我国企业遭受巨大损失。更为严重的是，近几年跨国公司不断加大专利战略布局，利用"专利先行"实现"跑马圈地"，通过早期的专利布局赢得市场竞争的先机，以专利为名的商业阻击战将越来越激烈。❶我国部分产业表面繁荣的背后承受着"国际市场边缘化"的困境，"专利诉讼""专利费用支出"在一定程度上阻止了企业良性发展。加入WTO后，中国市场开放度大大提高，低成本已经不再是中国企业独有的优势，

---

❶ 操秀英、何建昆："战略性新兴产业知识产权研究等待破题"，载《科技日报》2011年4月21日。

而自主知识产权将成为中国未来经济的主要增长点。❶
因此，我国应深入全面实施专利战略，建立较完善的专利法律和政策体系，增强全社会的专利意识，为战略性新兴产业健康发展提供制度保障，进而提升国家整体竞争力。

（2）运用专利制度是获得战略性新兴产业财富的重要途径。专利是战略性新兴产业相关企业的无形资产之一。高效的专利管理，尤其是专利战略管理能够通过引导创新方向和激励创新，有效发挥专利制度促进技术创新的重要作用。通过强化专利管理能力，优化专利战略能够大幅促进战略性新兴产业的专利创造、运用和保护水平，发挥相关技术资源优势，获得更多的高额利润，为相关企业创造更多的财富，促进战略性新兴产业健康发展。

（3）专利制度为战略性新兴产业技术创新提供不竭动力。战略性新兴产业是以技术创新为基础的技术密集型的新兴产业，具有较大的不确定性，不同类型的创新主体和投资者在培育和发展战略性新兴产业过程中，将不可避免地面临更多的风险性。但是如果战略性新兴产业相关企业拥有的技术能够获得充分的专利保护，这种

---

❶ 汤建辉："发展战略性新兴产业亟须知识产权保护"，载《湖北日报》2010年12月11日。

风险可能会在一定程度上得到降低，因此，有效的专利制度，尤其是高效的专利执法措施将为培育和发展战略性新兴产业提供保障，高效的专利保护管理水平则成为战略性新兴产业技术创新的不竭动力。

（4）专利制度是战略性新兴产业创新成果市场化的纽带。现代专利制度是市场经济的产物，它将有效推动战略性新兴产业技术创新、调整市场结构和增加产品竞争力，有效融合不同类型创新主体的技术创新水平和市场竞争能力，并通过产品市场创新资源配置。合理的专利制度能够有效促进战略性新兴产业技术专利的市场化和产业化，最终实现战略性新兴产业的快速发展。在这一过程中，专利制度通过将专利技术的市场化和产业化，成为战略性新兴产业创新成果市场化的纽带。

（5）专利制度是奠定战略性新兴产业优势的关键要素。创新主体拥有的专利数量，尤其是发明专利的申请量和授权量的多少，获得授权的专利质量的高低是战略性新兴产业发展的基础；市场主体将专利产业化的水平和程度以及其对专利许可、转让、质押、出资等运用能力的高低是战略性新兴产业发展的关键；政府对专利保护水平的高低以及执法力度的强弱是战略性新兴产业发展的前提。当然，不管是战略性新兴产业专利的创造、运用，还是战略性新兴产业专利的保护，都离不开对相关专利的高效管理。专利制度是专利管理的基础，所以市场主体将通过运用专利制度奠定战略性新兴产业的技术优势。

（6）专利制度是战略性新兴产业参与国际竞争的重要条件。战略性新兴产业是深度国际化的关键产业。该产业中的创新主体或者市场主体要想在创新环境开放、产业链布局以及创新资源全球配置的条件下获得竞争优势，只有在全球主要市场形成知识产权相对优势，才有可能取得整个产业的发展优势，从而保持其市场竞争力和可持续发展能力。[1] 健全的专利制度是一个国家或者地区保护技术创新的前提，也是参与国际技术竞争的重要条件。

3. 战略性新兴产业对专利制度运行的更高要求

创新是战略性新兴产业相关企业生存和发展的根本和源泉。技术含量高和高风险的特征决定了战略性新兴产业相关企业对创新成果高收益的预期。战略性新兴产业需要将自身发展特点和专利管理有机结合，将专利制度融入产业发展中，通过有效的专利管理机制实现企业的整体发展战略。与传统产业或成熟产业相比，新兴产业更需专利制度，其原因有以下三个方面。①战略性新兴产业市场的风险高。由于技术创新只有在创新过程

---

[1] 孟海燕："实施知识产权战略是培育和发展战略性新兴产业的关键"，载《中国发明与专利》2011年第9期，第17～18页。

完成并取得创新成果之后，才能形成产品并投入市场，市场需求的变化可能导致新产品市场效果达不到预期，这会给战略性新兴产业企业带来较大的市场风险。②战略性新兴产业企业平衡新结构与旧结构的难度较大。创新主体在某时点上作出发明并获得专利授权的概率，主要取决于其当时的研究团队及研发费用，而与过去的研发经验关系不大。专利制度有助于企业平衡新旧产品结构。③战略性新兴产业企业产品容易引起仿冒。专利保护制度为新兴技术公开可能带来的仿制风险提供保障。专利制度可以有效阻止竞争对手的"搭便车"行为，授予专利权人一定时期的市场垄断权利，从而使新兴企业收回前期投入和取得应有利润。❶ 具体而言，战略性新兴产业对知识产权管理提出如下新的要求。

（1）战略性新兴产业的科技性要求提升专利制度的保护强度。战略性新兴产业是新兴科技和新兴产业深度结合形成的，具有长期稳定的市场需求潜力，具有良好的经济、科技和社会效益，具有带动一批产业兴起，进而推动新一轮产业革命，最终形成战略性支柱产业的产业。大力发展战略性新兴产业是我国未来在激烈竞争的全球经济中取胜的主要策略。该策略关系到我国经济、

---

❶ 贾品荣："培育和发展新兴产业需要知识产权战略"，载《中国经济时报》2010年10月22日。

科技、文化和社会等多个领域能否可以科学发展。❶ 新兴产业要在日趋激烈的市场竞争中实现可持续发展，需要不断提升企业技术创新能力，争取更多的知识产权。企业技术创新的探索性强、周期性长、投资性大、技术复杂等特征决定了企业在专利的创造、获取、运营、保护各环节都存在较高的风险。拥有足够的发明专利等知识产权核心技术，具有较强的知识产权管理水平的新兴产业，才可以成为战略性新兴产业。

战略性新兴产业的技术密集型特征决定了其专利保护的重要性，或者说，战略性新兴产业发展与专利制度的健全程度具有非常紧密的相关性。在战略性新兴产业技术创新的创意酝酿阶段、技术研发阶段、产品开发和规模化生产阶段、战略布局等不同阶段提供帮助，提供对产业发展动向、科技发展趋势、市场需求前景等信息，同领域核心专利技术、主要专利技术和相关专利技术进行全面准确的检索、分析和评估等服务；帮助服务对象正确选择权利规避策略，确立研发方案，制定专利申请策略和专利布局规划，进行价值链分析，力求处于价值链的高端；帮助服务对象降低研发和产业化成本，

---

❶ 韩永进："城市创新经济结构体选择战略性新兴产业路线图研究"，见《2010年度京津冀区域协作论坛论文集》，第295～302页。

规避市场风险，追求经济价值和社会价值的最大化。❶
由专利制度对战略性新兴产业技术创新和产业发展的重
要性可以看出，健全和完善，乃至适度提高专利保护水
平对发展我国战略性新兴产业非常重要。

（2）战略性新兴产业的不确定性需要提升专利制
度的精度。战略性新兴产业发展的不确定性主要表现在
以下四个方面：①原始技术创新的不确定。原始技术创
新容易与传统观念及方法发生冲突，遇到困难，甚至失
败，需要长期探索和积累，整个过程充满不确定性。
②科技发展的不确定性。战略性新兴产业技术创新周期
长，培育过程核心技术难以确定，主流产品变化频繁，
技术创新的实用性和商业价值很难预估。③高科技人才
的不确定性。专业创新人才需要长期的技术和经验积
累，而具有一定积累的专业创新人才又易自创企业，新
兴企业面临核心人才流失的困境，很难形成稳定的产业
链，以最大化地将创新技术转化为商业价值。④外部竞
争的不确定性。由于专利具有排他性和独占性，许多企
业彼此追逐和竞争，竞争对手时时处于变动状态。以上
不确定性体现了战略性新兴产业面临的巨大风险，其专
利管理也必须要较高的精确度，能够覆盖产业发展的各

---

❶ 漆苏、朱雪忠、陈沁："企业自主创新中的专利风险评价研究"，载《情报
杂志》2009年第12期，第1~4页。

个环节。风险是无形的，是客观存在的，但在一定条件下有一定规律，具有可控性。企业可以通过设置有效的知识产权管理机构，实施知识产权管理制度，通过对知识产权风险的识别和评价等知识产权管理活动，降低、规避、转移和控制创新风险。❶ 更为重要的是，战略性新兴产业企业应该深刻认识这些风险，及早识别风险，有效运用专利制度应对相应风险。为了促进战略性新兴产业的快速发展，应该健全和完善专利制度，尤其是适度调整专利法实施细则，出台专门针对战略性新兴产业发展的产业政策，提高专利制度的精度。

（3）战略性新兴产业发展的竞争性要求专利制度的高效性。战略性新兴产业的技术密集型决定了其相关产品具有较高的附加值，可以为相关企业带来大量有形资产的同时，还可以为企业带来可观的无形财富。战略性新兴产业需要将新兴技术与产品相结合，实现其市场化和产业化，为企业带来更多的财富，从而可能引起竞争对手的模仿等侵犯知识产权的行为。从理论上讲，在这种情况下，知识产权制度就会有效阻止竞争对手的这种侵权行为，使新兴企业收回前期投入和取得应有利润。然而，因为在信息技术迅速发展的今天，战略性新兴产

---

❶ 漆苏、朱雪忠、陈沁："企业自主创新中的专利风险评价研究"，载《情报杂志》2009年第12期，第1~4页。

业相关产品信息传播非常迅速，公开方式多样化，加上战略性新兴产业的动态性、外部性和复杂性等特征，尤其是产品的可替代性强，企业竞争激烈，使得专利侵权行为发生的可能性大大增加。为了适应高速发展的技术革新，防止恶性竞争和垄断，保障市场主体的良性竞争环境，需要建立高效的专利管理制度与之相配套，有效提高专利制度保护战略性新兴产业发展的有效性。

（4）战略性新兴产业的战略性要求提升专利制度的高度。战略性新兴产业技术创新不仅关系未来主导产业的竞争水平，而且关系国家经济安全和国家竞争力的提高。把握全球产业调整机遇，统筹国内国际形势，要积极发展具有广阔市场前景、资源消耗低、带动系数大、就业机会多、综合效益好的战略性新兴产业，并在有基础、有条件的领域率先取得突破。但是战略性新兴产业的培育和发展受到市场前景、成长潜力、资源条件、产业结构等要素影响。在培育战略性新兴产业过程中，由于投资热情高、配套技术和基础设施发展不同步，往往会出现后续环节阶段性的"阻塞"和前端技术配套性的"过剩"现象。要科学分析新兴产业发展过程中的各种问题，把握好产业发展的规律和节奏，打通新兴产业发展各个环节间的障碍，促进战略性新兴产业发展。继续加大对前沿性、关键性、基础性和共性技术研究的支持力度，把自主创新政策的着力点聚焦到支持产品研发的前端和推广应用的后端上，创新适应新兴产业发展的商业模式，为自主创新产品打开市场做好服务工作。❶ 要达到上述要求，必须对战略性新兴产业中的技术、产品等进行高强度和高效率的专利管理。因此，为了真正把战略性新兴产业摆在国家经济发展的战略性地位，要科学分析战略性新兴产业自主创新过程所面临的背景和各种问题，把握好产业自主创新的规律和机制，实施专利战略，建立科学的专利管理制度，对相关专利进行科学管理，才能真正促进战略性新兴产业快速健康发展。

（三）小　结

战略性新兴产业是指我国在改革开放新时期作出的新的科技战略部署，是当今世界科学技术发展的前沿和方向，是新兴科技和新兴产业的深度融合，具有科技性、长远性、导向性、全局性和动态性等产业特征，关系到我国经济产业结构的优化升级和经济发展方式转变，对国民经济和社会发展具有战略支撑作用，最终发展成为提升我国综合国力和促进社会进步的先导产业、主导产业和支柱产业的新兴业态形式。它包括节能环保、新一代信息技术、生物产业、高端装备制造、新能

---

❶　万钢："把握全球产业调整机遇培育和发展战略性新兴产业"，载《求是》2010年第1期，第28～30页。

源、新材料和新能源汽车等七大产业，具有不确定性、战略性、政策导向性、外部性、创新性和复杂性等产业特征。专利制度对战略性新兴产业的发展具有新作用；专利制度是战略性新兴产业健康发展的重要保障；运用专利制度是获得战略性新兴产业财富的重要途径；专利保护制度为战略性新兴产业发展提供不竭动力；专利制度是战略性新兴产业创新成果市场化的纽带；专利制度是奠定战略性新兴产业优势的关键要素；专利制度是战略性新兴产业参与国际竞争的重要条件。同时，战略性新兴产业发展引发专利竞争新趋势；战略性新兴产业的科技性要求强化专利制度的强度；战略性新兴产业的不确定性需要提升专利制度的精度；战略性新兴产业发展的竞争性要求专利制度的高效性；战略性新兴产业的战略性要求提升专利制度的高度。

三、我国战略性新兴产业
授权发明专利整体发展趋势

　　发展战略性新兴产业是我国转变经济发展模式、调整产业结构的重要措施，而专利制度是保障战略性新兴产业健康、持续发展的核心制度之一。2013年战略性新兴产业实现较快增长，全年节能环保、生物、新一代信息技术以及新能源等领域重点产业主营业务收入达到16.7万亿元，同比增长15.6%，高于工业总体11.2%的增速；产业经济效益良好，全年重点产业利润总额达7 643.2亿元，同比增长20.7%，明显高于工业总体12.2%的增速。战略性新兴产业继续成为社会资本追逐的热点领域，2013年年末，战略性新兴产业A股上市公司总市值占总体市值的比重达20.7%，较2012年年末提升5.8个百分点。❶以专利数据为基础的战略性新兴产业专利指标直接反映了这些产业技术创新水平，统计和分析这些产业相关技术领域专利数据可以在一定程度上明确战略性新兴产业

---

　　❶　国家信息中心信息资源开发部："战略性新兴产业2013年发展形势及2014年展望"，载http://www.sic.gov.cn/News/82/2591.htm，2014-05-31。

的创新态势，发现这些产业不同技术领域中的优势和存在问题，对相关技术领域提出专利技术预警管理，为制定相关政策提供参考依据，引导和支持战略性新兴产业快速发展。

本部分主要明确或分析以下问题：（1）战略性新兴产业主要产业与专利国际分类号（IPC）对应统计；（2）战略性新兴产业及其各产业授权发明专利变化趋势；（3）战略性新兴产业及其各产业国内外创新主体在我国授权发明专利趋势；（4）战略性新兴产业国外创新主体在我国授权发明专利分布以及国内创新主体在我国授权发明专利地区分布。

（一）战略性新兴产业分类与
专利国际分类号对应统计

为了更好地运用专利数据反映战略性新兴产业技术创新和技术保护情况，国家知识产权局规划发展司组织将战略性新兴产业分类与IPC进行对照研究，建立战略性新兴产业分类与IPC对照关系，并形成对照关系表，作为研究战略性新兴产业专利技术相关研究的基础。为了缩减篇幅，本研究报告此处仅列出七大战略性新兴产业分类的简单层级及IPC对应条数情况（见表3-1）。在研究报告相关部分就重点分析产业涉及技术专利分类号进行专门说明。

从表3-1可以看出，首先，在七大战略性新兴产业中，节能环保产业、新一代信息技术产业和新材料产业涉及的IPC最多，分别为1 511条、1 045条和1 054条，说明这些产业专利技术分布最为复杂；其次是新能源汽车产业、高端装备制造产业和生物产业涉及的IPC相对较多，分别为750条、684条和611条，说明这些产业专利技术分布相对复杂；最后，新能源产业涉及的IPC最少，只有345条，说明该产业专利技术分布相对简单。

表3-1　战略性新兴产业分类与国际专利分类（IPC）对应条数统计[❶]

战略性新兴产业分类				对IPC（类）
第一层产业分类代码	第一层产业分类名称	第二层产业分类代码	第二层产业分类名称	
1	节能环保产业	1.1	高效节能产业	433
		1.2	先进环保产业	537
		1.3	资源循环利用产业	541
			合计	1 511

❶ 国家知识产权局："战略性新兴产业发明专利统计分析总报告"，载http://www.sipo.gov.cn/tjxx/，2014-06-01。

战略性新兴产业分类				对IPC（类）
第一层产业分类代码	第一层产业分类名称	第二层产业分类代码	第二层产业分类名称	
2	新一代信息技术产业	2.1	下一代信息网络产业	130
		2.2	电子核心基础产业	764
		2.3	高端软件和新型信息技术服务	151
			合计	1 045
3	生物产业	3.1	生物制品制造产业	380
		3.2	生物工程设备制造产业	125
		3.3	生物技术应用产业	106
			合计	611
4	高端装备制造产业	4.1	航空装备产业	128
		4.2	卫星及应用产业	123
		4.3	轨道交通装备产业	141
		4.4	海洋工程装备产业	56
		4.5	智能制造装备产业	236
			合计	684
5	新能源产业	5.1	核电产业	64
		5.2	风能产业	44
		5.3	太阳能产业	126
		5.4	生物质能及其他新能源产业	78
		5.5	智能电网产业	33
			合计	345

续表

战略性新兴产业分类				对IPC（类）
第一层产业分类代码	第一层产业分类名称	第二层产业分类代码	第二层产业分类名称	
6	新材料产业	6.1	新型功能材料产业	385
		6.2	先进结构材料产业	276
		6.3	高性能复合材料产业	269
		6.4	前沿新材料产业	124
			合计	1 054
7	新能源汽车	7.1	新能源汽车整车制造	339
		7.2	新能源汽车装置、配件制造	372
		7.3	新能源汽车相关设施及服务	39
			合计	750
		合计		6 000

（二）战略性新兴产业及各产业授权发明专利变化趋势

1. 战略性新兴产业授权发明专利整体变化趋势

2008年以来，随着国家相关政策的实施，我国战略性新兴产业发展迅速，发明专利授权量快速增长，年均增长率达到26.04%，高于同期发明专利授权量的年均增长率23.37%。图3-1反映的是2008～2012年我国战略性新兴产业授权发明专利变化趋势。从图3-1中至少可以得出三点结论：（1）2008～2012年我国战略性新兴产业授权发明专利数量整体增加趋势明显，但不同年份增长率差异较大；（2）2008～2009年我国战略性新兴产业授权发明专利增长率最高（42.98%）；（3）2009～2010年授权发明专利增长率最低（1.35%）。

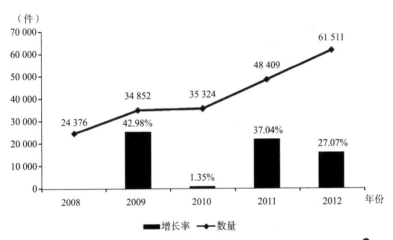

图3-1 2008～2012年战略性新兴产业授权发明专利变化趋势[1]

2. 战略性新兴产业各产业授权发明专利变化趋势

因为战略性新兴产业技术特征、涉及国际专利分类情况以及产业发展基础不同，所以七大战略性新兴产业

---

[1] 本部分图形数据来源均见国家知识产权局："战略性新兴产业发明专利统计分析总报告"，载http://www.sipo.gov.cn/tjxx/，2014-06-01。

授权发明专利数量不同不难理解。图3-2表示2008～2012年七大战略性新兴产业各自授权发明专利变化情况。从图3-2可以看出，尽管2008～2012年各产业授权发明专利量不断增长，但是各产业授权发明专利数量基础及其增长率差异较大。具体而言，节能环保产业、新一代信息技术产业和生物产业授权发明专利基础较好，发展速度较快，尤其是新一代信息技术产业，表现突出；高端装备制造产业、新能源产业和新材料产业授权发明专利数量较弱，增长较慢；新能源汽车产业授权发明专利基础最弱，增长率也最低。

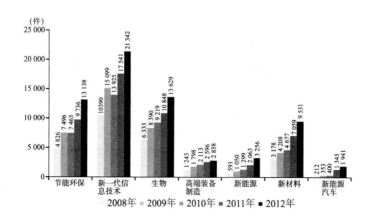

图3-2 2008～2012年战略性新兴产业各产业授权发明专利量变化

（三）战略性新兴产业及各产业国内外
授权发明专利变化趋势

1. 战略性新兴产业国内外创新主体授权发明专利整
体变化趋势

国内外不同国籍的创新主体在我国获得发明专利的
数量和质量情况反映了其各自在我国相关技术领域的优
势。图3-3反映了2011～2012年战略性新兴产业国内外创
新主体在我国获得发明专利授权情况，也反映了国内创
新主体与国外创新主体在战略性新兴产业技术领域的专
利技术优势。

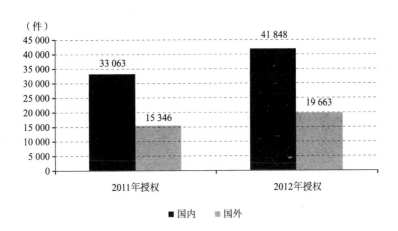

图3-3 战略性新兴产业国内外创新主体在我国授权发明专利变化

从图3-3中至少可以发现：国内外创新主体战略性新兴产业技术领域在我国获得发明专利的授权量都在大幅度增长，但是国外创新主体战略性新兴产业技术领域在我国获得授权的发明专利增长率比国内创新主体高。可见，国内战略性新兴产业发明专利授权的增幅既低于同期国内发明专利授权的增幅，又低于战略性新兴产业国外在华发明专利的增幅，发明专利授权增速优势尚未显现。

2. 战略性新兴产业各产业国内外创新主体授权发明专利变化趋势

图3-4反映的是2011年与2012年战略性新兴产业各产业国内外创新主体在我国获得发明专利的授权数量比值变化情况。尽管图3-3说明国内外创新主体在我国发明专利授权总量在较大幅度增长，但是从图3-4可以发现，不同类型战略性新兴产业国内外创新主体在我国授权发明专利数量比值变化存在较大差异。其中高端装备制造产业和新能源汽车产业的国内外创新主体在我国获得授权发明专利数量比值增长较大；生物产业和新能源产业国内外创新主体在我国获得授权发明专利数量比值下降幅度较大；节能环保产业和新一代信息技术产业国内外创新主体在我国获得授权发明专利数量比值增长幅度较小；新材料产业国内外创新主体在我国获得授权发明专

利数量比值小幅减少。

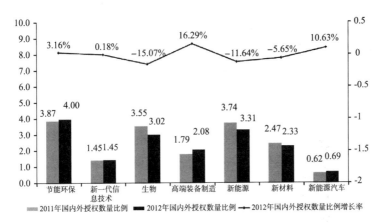

图3-4 战略性新兴产业各产业国内外创新主体在我国授权发明专利
数量比例变化

（四）战略性新兴产业授权发明专利
国外区域及国内地区分布

1.战略性新兴产业国外创新主体在我国授权发明专
利分布

国外不同国家或地区的创新主体在我国获得发明专
利授权情况直接反映该国或者地区在我国专利技术的布
局情况。图3-5表示2012年战略性新兴产业国外创新主体
在我国授权发明专利分布情况。从图3-5可知，日本和美
国的创新主体对我国战略性新兴产业发明专利布局相当

重视，两国发明专利授权量之和占国外创新主体获得授权发明专利比例的64%多，这一现象值得我们关注。其次是韩国、德国和法国在我国对战略性新兴产业进行了一定比例的投入和专利布局。

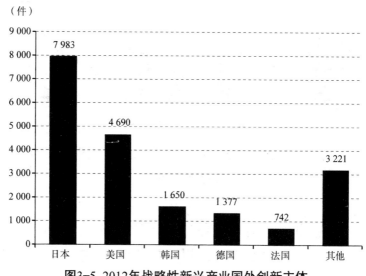

图3-5 2012年战略性新兴产业国外创新主体
在我国授权发明专利分布

2. 战略性新兴产业国内创新主体在我国授权发明专利分布

我国地域辽阔，经济发展和科技水平差异较大，所以不同地区在战略性新兴产业获得授权发明专利比例存在差异在所难免。图3-6反映2012年战略性新兴产业国内创新主体获得授权发明专利地区分布情况。

从图3-6可知，我国国内创新主体在战略性新兴产业中获得的发明专利授权量呈现明显的东西差异现象。即从国内战略性新兴产业发明专利授权的地域分布来看，东部同中西部地区差异十分明显，这与我国经济结构的特点基本吻合。东部地区在战略性新兴产业发明专利授权中占绝对主力地位。中部地区、西部地区在国内战略性新兴产业发明专利授权中所占比重相对较低。

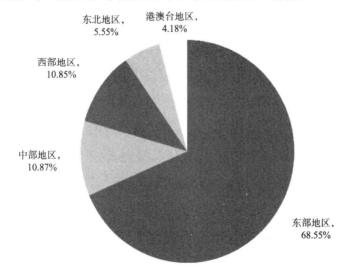

图3-6 2012年战略性新兴产业国内创新主体授权发明专利地区分布

（五）小 结

通过对战略性新兴产业在我国获得授权的发明专利相关问题研究，本研究报告得出以下六点结论：（1）我国战略性新兴产业授权发明专利数量整体增加趋势明显，但不同年份增长率差异较大；（2）尽管战略性新兴产业各产业授权发明专利量不断增长，但是各产业授权发明专利数量基础及其增长率差异较大；（3）国内战略性新兴产业发明专利授权的增幅既低于同期国内发明专利授权的增幅，又低于战略性新兴产业国外在华发明专利的增幅，发明专利授权增速优势尚未显现；（4）不同类型战略性新兴产业国内外创新主体在我国授权发明专利数量比值变化存在较大差异；（5）日本和美国的创新主体对我国战略性新兴产业发明专利布局优势相当明显；（6）我国国内创新主体在战略性新兴产业中获得的发明专利授权量呈现明显的东西差异现象。因为七大战略性新兴产业技术特征、前期发展基础、产业政策以及与专利制度的依赖程度均存在一定差异，所以如果对专利制度促进我国战略性新兴产业发展问题一概而论，很难进行较为深入且具有针对性的研究，因此本研究报告以下部分进行个别产业个别问题的专门研究。

四、我国战略性新兴产业发明专利及其结构现状与问题*
——以"节能环保产业"为例**

当前，全球环境问题突出，能源资源紧缺，制约人类经济社会的发展。在缓解资源环境对人类经济社会发展的制约及降低人类对自然资源的依赖的背景下，发展节能环保产业非常重要，因此，节能环保产业成为我国加快培育和发展的七大战略性新兴产业之一。❶ 发展节能环保产业，一方面为缓解传统能源消耗压力，实现我国"十二五"节能减排约束性目标提供坚实的产业和技术支撑；另一方面对我国扩大有效需求，转变经济发展方式，促进产业转型升级，培育新经济增长点和新兴支柱产业具有重要意义。

---

  * 本小节内容由乔永忠和梁齐共同创作完成。

  ** 这种研究方法存在很大局限性，如战略性新兴产业七大产业各个产业对专利制度的依赖性差异决定了专利制度对七大战略性新兴产业的作用不同，节能环保产业对战略性新兴产业的代表性问题有待进一步分析，此处选择研究视角的目的是，为了研究问题更加深入具体，而不至过于笼统，同时需要说明的是，这种研究视角仍然处于中间或者宏观阶段，这一研究方向有待于更加深入的研究，如更为具体的产业技术等。第五、第六部分与此类似。

  ❶ 国务院："'十二五'国家战略性新型产业发展规划"，2010年。

　　节能环保产业的发展离不开技术创新，专利是衡量技术创新最可靠、最直接的指标之一，专利技术的态势分布不仅能够反映产业最新的研发趋势，也有利于企业制定最佳的技术战略。专利制度通过"技术开发—保护—利用—改进—保护—利用"不断循环过程，提高社会的节能环保技术创新能力。为此，2012年，国家知识产权局对低碳、节能等绿色技术的发明专利申请实施优先审查制度。绿色科技专利优先审查制度将有利于节能环保技术产业化经营，进一步促进节能环保产业的创新与发展。

　　自2010年国家将节能环保产业列入我国加快培育和发展的七大战略性新兴产业以来，与节能环保技术及产业相关的研究越来越受到国内外学者的重视。现有研究在产业的发展与趋势、策略与措施、经验与创新等方面进行了值得借鉴的研究工作，但大多从宏观角度进行定性分析，对节能环保产业发明专利的实证研究结果相对较少。而对授权专利的实证分析研究有利于明晰中国节能环保技术创新能力差异及与国外在该产业中的差距，更好地制定产业发展策略。

　　专利发展态势是衡量一个产业发展的重要指标，采用专利指标对产业技术水平和创新能力进行量化分析是一种新的研究趋势，与产业技术相关专利文献的稳健指数增长的特征分析是判断产业技术创新活动最常见的方法。基于此，为明晰我国节能环保产业技术领域发展特点，促进节能环保产业发展，本部分采用专利文献计量的方法，定量分析我国节能环保产业相关技术发展现状与趋势，为促进节能环保产业技术发展提供借鉴。

（一）节能环保产业发展及研究现状

近年来，我国节能环保产业发展迅速。2010年，国家将环保产业列为战略性新兴产业重点发展后，节能环保产业总产值达2万亿元，从业人数达到2 800万人。❶ 2013年节能环保产业在政策的带动之下，延续了良好的发展势头，规模继续扩张，全年增速在20%以上。其中，环保产业继续强劲发展势头，2013年环保专用设备和监测仪器产业主营业务收入超过2 200亿元，同比增速达22.1%。节能产业发展成绩显著，节能服务产业总产值从2012年的1 653.4亿元增长到2 155.6亿元，增幅达30.4%；合同能源管理投资从2012年557.7亿元增长到742.3亿元，增幅为33.1%，相应实现的节能量达2 559.7万吨标准煤，减排二氧化碳6 399.3万吨。❷ 节能环保产业的发展离不开技术的创新，为了促进节能环保产业的

---

❶ 国务院："'十二五'节能环保产业发展规划"，2010年。
❷ 国家信息中心信息资源开发部："战略性新兴产业2013年发展形势及2014年展望"，载http://www.sic.gov.cn/News/82/2591.htm，2014-05-31。

发展，各省市相继出台一系列措施促进技术创新，鼓励发明创造，使得我国的节能环保技术呈跨越式发展。技术创新与该技术领域专利的发展状况在一定程度上存在正相关关系。专利是衡量一个产业发展状况的最直接的指标之一，❶ 能够反映最新的产业研发趋势。因此，通过对节能环保产业中相关技术专利发展状况的分析能更直观反映出我国节能环保产业的技术发展水平和趋势，甚至整个产业的发展状况。专利能保护节能环保产业中的环境友好型技术，促进产业的创新与发展。❷

近年来，我国的节能环保技术的专利申请量及所获的授权量逐年递增，节能环保技术专利申请量及拥有量的大幅提高大大促进了我国节能环保产业的发展。2012年节能环保产业国内发明专利授权量前十位的省市包括北京、江苏、广东、浙江、山东、上海、辽宁、湖南、河南和湖北。这些排序前十位的省市节能环保产业发明专利授权量共计7 507 件，占节能环保产业国内来源的发明专利授权总量的71.4%。2011年和2012年，节能环保产业国内发明专利授权量的国内排名前十位的省市分布情

---

❶ Janghyeok Yoon, Kwangsoo Kim b: "An analysis of property-function based patent networks for strategic R&D planning in fast-moving industries: The case of silicon-based thin film solar cells", *Expert Systems with Applications*, 2012, (39):4409 ~ 7717.

❷ Bronwyn H. Hall, Christian Helmers: "Innovation and diffusion of clean/green technology: Can patent commons help", *Journal of Environmental Economics and Management*, 2013, (66):33 ~ 51.

况变化不大，入围省市未发生变化，只是若干省市相对的排序位置出现了一些调整（上海与山东的排序互换，辽宁与湖南的排序互换，湖北与河南的排序互换）。前三甲均依次为北京、江苏、广东，2011年、2012 年它们的节能环保产业发明专利授权量分别为2 646 件、2 061 件和1 668 件，三省市的发明专利授权量之和占整个产业国内发明专利授权量的34.8%。❶

虽然我国的节能环保技术的专利发展态势良好，但在该领域开展的研究成果并不多，节能环保产业的发展也缺乏足够的理论支持。通过在"中国知网（CNKI）"对"节能环保"及"专利"等相关关键词的检索，除了对战略性新兴产业技术专利相关问题的个别研究成果外，专门针对节能环保产业的专利分析研究成果并不多，且都集中在某一省市或节能环保技术某个技术领域的专利分析研究，统计数据年限较早。如江苏省，1985～2004年，节能环保技术的发明专利主要来自南京、无锡及苏州等工业发展较好的城市，技术领域主要集中于污水治理方面。❷ 而在对粤港澳环保产业专利态势分析中，环保专利主要集中于珠三角区域，港澳在该

---

❶ 国家知识产权局规划发展司："战略性新兴产业授权发明专利统计报告"，载《专利统计简报》2013 年第11 期，第34页。

❷ 唐宝莲："江苏省环保领域专利开发利用活动分析"，载《江苏科技信息》2005年第8期，第28～29页。

产业的专利申请及拥有量上均亟须提高；广东省环保产业中的专利申请主要来自水污染治理、空气污染治理及固体废弃物处理等技术领域，且该产业的核心技术基本被日本、美国等专利强国所掌握。[1] 为明晰我国节能环保技术发展的特点，并为我国的节能环保产业的发展提供更宽领域的理论支持，本部分从节能环保产业专利区域分布及技术领域布局分析我国节能环保产业发明专利的发展态势，从而为我国节能环保产业的投资发展提供借鉴。

（二）数据来源和专利分类

本部分所有的统计数据是采自"专利之星专利检索系统"平台（http://searchtel. patentstar.com.cn/），检索时间段为2008～2013年。通过对节能环保产业所涉及发明专利IPC分类号进行授权量检索并对各相关数据归类整合及分析。我国节能环保产业按技术类型可分为节能、资源循环利用和环境治理产业，其涉及的主要技术领域及专利IPC分类号，依据《战略性新兴产业专利检索手册》确定，涉及的主要技术领域及专利的IPC分类号如表4-1

---

❶ 魏庆华、张新明："粤港澳环保产业专利态势分析与对策研究"，载《广东科技》2003年第7期，第74～76页。

所示。❶

表4-1 节能环保产业涉及的主要技术领域及IPC分类号

类别	子技术领域	涉及IPC分类号
节能类	高效工业锅炉设计制造技术	F22B9/00−F22B9/18;F22B27/00−F22B27/16; F22B29/00−F22B29/12
	余热余能利用技术	F27D17/00
	高效环保空调与热泵技术	F24F1/00−F24F1/04;F24F3/00−F24F3/16;F24F5/00;F25B30/00−F25B30/06
资源循环利用类	低品位金属矿回收利用技术	B03B7/00;B03B9/06;B03D1/00−B03D1/26
	脱硫石膏综合利用技术	C04B7/04;C04B11/00−C04B11/30;C04B28/14−C04B28/16
	煤矸综合利用技术	C04B18/04−C04B18/12;C10L5/48
	餐厨垃圾处理与综合利用技术	B09B1/00;B09B3/00;A23K1/10
	废旧物质拆解分拣处理技术	B29B17/00−B29B17/02;H01M6/25;H01M10/54;H01J9/52
	再创造关键技术	C05F9/00−C05F9/04;B22F8/00
	城市污水污泥资源化技术	C02F11/00C02F11/02;C05F7/00−C05F7/04

❶ 节能环保产业涉及的IPC分类号采用由湖南省知识产权局组织编写的《战略性新兴产业专利检索手册》（知识产权出版社2013年版）所提供的IPC分类号。

续表

类别	子技术领域	涉及IPC分类号
环境治理类	重金属废水、废气、废渣污染控制技术	C02F1/62−C02F1/64;B01D53/64
	烟气脱硫脱硝关键技术	B01D53/48−B01D53/60
	高浓度有机废水控制技术	C02F1/00−C02F1/78;C02F3/00−C02F3/34; C02F9/00−C02F9/14
	重金属、持久性有机污染物污染土壤修复技术	B09C1/00−B09C1/10

（三）节能环保产业授权发明专利布局

1.节能环保产业三大技术领域发明专利授权量分布

通过统计我国节能环保产业近6年的发明专利授权量，可以得出该产业专利技术发展的现状和趋势。图4-1显示的是2008～2013年中国节能环保产业发明专利授权量的变化趋势，从中可以看出我国节能环保产业技术发明授权量的变化特点。首先，2008～2013年三大技术领域授权发明专利总数均有增加，但增加幅度不同，环境治理技术领域增加幅度最大，节能技术领域增加幅度最小；其次，2008～2010年三大技术领域授权发明专利增加幅度均不大，但2010～2013年趋势明显不同，环境治理技术领域授权发明专利数量猛增，资源循环利用技术领域次之，而节能技术领域在2011年的授权发明专利数出现略微降低情况；最后，环境治理技术领域授权发明专利明显比资源循环利用和节能技术领域具有优势，而资源循环利用和节能两个技术领域授权发明专利数变化趋势差异不是很明显。可见，节能环保产业中环境治理技术领域创新能力要明显强于资源循环利用和节能两个技术领域。

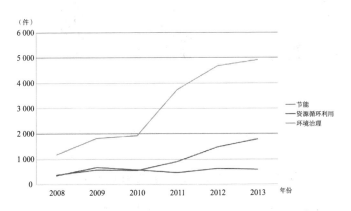

图4-1 节能环保产业发明专利授权量的变化趋势

2. 节能环保产业三大技术领域国内外专利授权量分布

2008～2013年国家知识产权局授权的节能环保产业三大领域国内外发明专利分布如图4-2所示，从中可以发现如下两个特征：（1）三大领域国内授权发明专利数均占优势，即国内在三大技术领域中均有明显技术优势，国外专利权人对相关技术领域产业发展威胁不大；（2）不同技术的技术优势度不同，环境治理技术领域优势明显，资源循环利用技术领域优势略微次之，节能技术领域国内专利技术优势相对较弱。

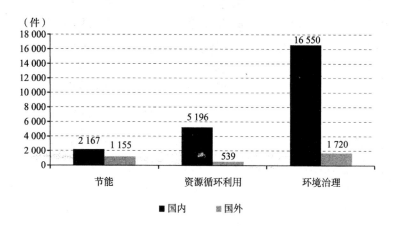

图4-2 节能环保产业三大技术领域国内外专利授权量分布

3. 我国节能环保产业发明专利地区布局

2008～2013年，国家知识产权局授予节能环保技术专利共27 327件，其中国内23 913件，国外3 414件。如表4-2所示，国内节能环保产业发明专利授权量排名前十的省市分别是北京、江苏、浙江、广东、上海、山东、天津、湖北、辽宁、湖南。该十省市总共获得18 015件发明专利授权，占近6年国内在该产业技术专利授权量的75.3%。在国外所获专利授权中，共有40多个国家或地区获得我国节能环保产业技术发明专利的授权，其中日本所获的授权量最多，共1 472件，占国外所获授权量的43.1%，其后依次是韩国、美国、德国、法国、荷兰、加拿大、英国、瑞士、澳大利亚，国外排名前十的国家共获该产业专利授权3 067件，占国外所获授权总量的90%以上。

由表4-2可以看出：（1）我国节能环保产业地区发展严重不均衡。2008～2013年我国节能环保产业技术发明专利的授权主要集中于北京及东部沿海地区，中西部经济欠发达地区的节能环保产业的专利申请量及拥有量都远远低于东部沿海地区，东部发达地区是我国节能环保产业集中地，是支撑该产业发展的重要力量。（2）随着中西部经济的发展，节能环保产业的省市竞争将更加激烈，湖南、湖北等中部省份已在东部省市中成功突围，产业技术发明专利所获的授权量都进入了前十位。（3）我国节能环保技术发明专利的国外申请授权集中于日本、韩国、美国、欧盟等四个国家或地区。其中，日本、韩国、美国三国在我国节能环保技术产业中优势地位明显。

表4-2 2008～2013年我国节能环保产业发明
专利国内外区域布局（前十名） （件）

排名	国内		国外	
	省（市）	数量	国家（地区）	数量
1	北京	3 673	日本	1 472
2	江苏	3 184	韩国	565
3	浙江	2 108	美国	476
4	广东	2 060	德国	182
5	上海	1 986	法国	107
6	山东	1 464	荷兰	68
7	天津	1 105	加拿大	57
8	湖北	877	英国	56
9	辽宁	842	瑞士	43
10	湖南	716	澳大利亚	41

（四）节能产业技术领域专利布局

节能产业主要技术领域包括高效工业锅炉设计制造技术（F22B9/00-F22B9/18；F22B27/00-F22B27/16；F22B29/00-F22B29/12）、余热余能利用技术（F27D17/00）、高效环保空调与热泵技术（F24F1/00-F24F1/04；F24F3/00-F24F3/16；F24F5/00；F25B30/00-F25B30/06）。

1. 节能产业主要技术领域发明专利授权量总体布局

2008～2013年节能环保产业中节能产业的主要技术领域发明专利授权量总体布局如图4-3所示。

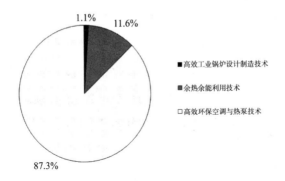

图4-3 节能产业主要技术领域发明专利授权量总体布局

从图4-3中可以发现该领域发明创造主要集中在高效环保空调与热泵技术领域，该技术领域的专利授权量为2 899件，占专利授权总量的87.3%；余热余能技术次之，共有388件发明专利获授权；而高效工业锅炉设计制造技术的发明专利的授权量最少，6年间总共才有35件专利授权。由图4-3可以发现两个特征：（1）2008～2013年，我国节能产业的发明专利授权量分布严重不平衡，主要集中于高效环保空调与热泵技术，余热余能利用技术和高效锅炉技术的发明创造力仍有待提升；（2）我国节能产业中高效环保空调与热泵技术竞争激烈。

2．节能产业主要技术领域国内外发明专利授权量布局

从中国节能产业主要技术领域国内外授权专利分布情况（见图4-4）中可以发现以下特征：（1）我国节能

产业中的国内外技术领域专利授权量的布局情况大体一致，均以极高的比例集中于高效环保空调与热泵技术，而余热余能利用技术及高效工业锅炉设计制造技术均占较小的比例；（2）我国节能产业各技术领域中，国内所获专利授权量在绝对值上均多于国外，但国内外相差的倍数不相同，余热余能利用技术国内外相差的倍数最大，约达7倍，其他两个技术领域维持在1.7倍左右。这表明在与国外横向对比时，我国余热余能利用技术的创新能力更强。由此可以得出结论：我国节能产业各技术领域的专利授权量国内外的分布情况基本一致，而国内的余热余能利用技术的发展更有优势。

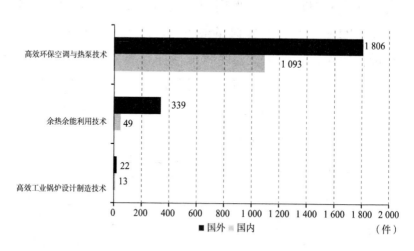

图4-4 节能产业主要技术领域国内外授权专利分布

（五）资源循环利用产业技术领域专利布局

资源循环利用产业主要技术领域包括低品位金属矿回收利用技术（B03B7/00；B03B9/06；B03D1/00-B03D1/26）、脱硫石膏综合利用技术（C04B7/04；C04B11/00-C04B11/30C04B28/14-C04B28/16）、煤矸综合利用技术（C04B18/04-C04B18/12；C10L5/48）、餐厨垃圾处理与综合利用技术（B09B1/00；B09B3/00；A23K1/10）、废旧物质拆解分拣处理技术（B29B17/00-B29B17/02；H01M6/25；H01M10/54；H01J9/52）、再创造关键技术（C05F9/00-C05F9/04；B22F8/00）、城市污水污泥资源化技术（C02F11/00-C02F11/02；C05F7/00-C05F7/04）等。

1.资源循环利用产业主要技术领域授权发明专利总体布局

2008～2012年中国资源循环利用产业各相关技术专利授权量布局（见图4-5）具有以下特征：（1）我国资源循环利用产业发明专利的授权量主要集中于与人类社会生活密切相关的餐厨垃圾处理与综合利用技术和城市污水污泥资源化技术；（2）低品位金属矿回收利用技术、脱硫石膏综合利用技术及煤矸综合利用技术等工业生产与应用技术的发明专利授权量分别比较均匀；（3）废旧物质拆散分拣处理技术和再创造技术的发明力最薄弱，所获专利授权量较少，未能发挥出其在资源循环利用产业中应有的作用。

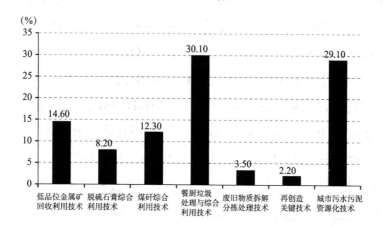

图4-5 资源循环利用产业各相关技术专利授权量布局

可见，中国资源循环利用产业中，餐厨垃圾处理与综合利用技术和城市污水污泥资源化技术是该产业的龙头技术力量，而再创造关键技术和废旧物质拆解分拣处理技术较薄弱。

2. 资源循环利用产业主要技术领域国内外发明专利授权量布局

图4-6反映了我国资源循环利用产业主要技术领域授权的国内外发明专利分布情况。

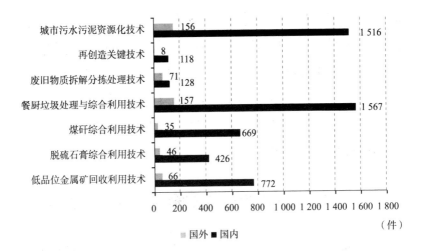

图4-6 资源循环利用产业主要技术领域国内外发明专利授权量分布

从图4-6可以看出资源循环利用产业主要技术领域国内外发明专利授权量分布存在以下特点：（1）资源循环利用产业中，各技术领域的国内发明专利的授权量均远高于国外；（2）餐厨垃圾处理与综合利用技术及城市污水污泥资源化技术是国内外创新主体研发的重点技术领域，所获的发明专利授权量最多，再创造关键技术无论在国内或国外所获的授权量均最少；（3）国内外各技术领域的发明专利授权量在产业中各自的排位不一致。国内发明专利授权中煤矸综合利用技术占国内专利授权量的比率较大，排名靠前，国外却排在倒数第二位；国外排名中，废旧物质拆解分拣技术所获专利授权量排在第三位，而国内排在倒数第二位。这表明，相对而言，国内对煤矸综合利用技术仍然有较强的创新能力，而国外对废旧物质拆解分拣技术发明创造更活跃。

可见，餐厨垃圾处理与综合利用技术及城市污水污泥资源化技术是资源循环利用产业中国内外主要的创新技术领域，煤矸石膏综合利用技术仍然是我国资源循环利用产业中重要的创新领域。

（六）环境治理产业技术领域专利布局分析

环境治理产业的主要技术领域包括重金属废水、废气、废渣污染控制技术（C02F1/62–C02F1/64；B01D53/64），烟气脱硫脱硝关键技术（B01D53/48–B01D53/60），高浓度有机废水控制技术（C02F1/00–C02F1/78；C02F3/00–C02F3/34；C02F9/00–C02F9/14）以及重金属、持久性有机污染物污染土壤修复技术（B09C1/00–B09C1/10）等。

1. 环境治理产业主要技术领域授权发明专利总体布局

图4-7反映了我国环境治理产业主要技术领域授权发明专利总体布局。

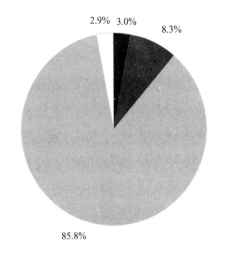

2.9% 3.0% 8.3%

■ 重金属废水、废气、废渣污染控制技术

■ 烟气脱硫脱硝关键技术

▨ 高浓度有机废水控制技术

□ 重金属、持久性有机污染物污染土壤修复技术

85.8%

图4-7 资源循环利用产业主要技术领域授权发明专利总体布局

从图4-7可以发现，2008～2013年我国环境治理产业共获得18 270件发明专利授权，产业内各技术领域专利授权量分布严重不均衡，八成以上的专利授权量集中于高浓度有机废水控制技术。高浓度有机废水控制技术拥有较高专利授权量，从技术层面说明工业有机废水实现问题的严峻性刺激着该领域的技术创新。重金属废水、废气、废渣污染控制技术及重金属、持久有机污染物污染土壤恢复技术的持续创新力不足，分别仅占该产业授权总量的3%左右。由此可知，在我国环境治理产业中，高浓度有机废水控制技术是该产业最集中的创新领域，而重金属废水、废气、废渣污染控制技术及重金属、持久性有机污染物污染土壤恢复技术的创新力量仍需大力提高。

2. 环境治理产业主要技术领域国内外发明专利授权量布局

从中国环境治理产业主要技术领域国内外发明专利授权量布局（见图4-8）可以发现以下特征：（1）环境治理产业中，国内各相关技术领域发明专利的授权量远多于国外；（2）国内外专利授权量的布局情况基本一致，均大幅度集中于高浓度有机废水控制技术上，这表明工业高浓度有机废水控制技术是我国的环境治理的重点技术领域。

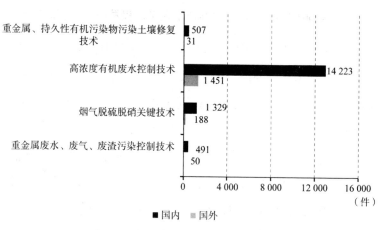

图4-8 环境治理产业主要技术领域国内外发明专利授权量分布

（七）国内外特定专业技术领域发明专利分布状况

每一件专利文件都会按照IPC分类，以说明所涉及的具体技术领域。统计专利文件的IPC分类号分布，可以发现技术创新集中的技术领域和技术创新能力的大小。与国别相结合，可以观察国内外在不同技术领域中的分布，确定特定技术领域国内外的竞争程度。表4-3反映的是2008～2013年节能环保技术发明专利国内外授权量特定专业技术分布情况。根据表4-3可以得出，2008～2013年我国节能环保产业国内外发明专利授权量排名情况具有以下特点：（1）C02F1/00-C02F1/78（水、废水或污水的处理技术）这一特定技术领域的发明专利的国内外发明专利授权量均排名第一，成为国内外技术创新的重点领域。（2）我国节能环保产业特定专业技术领域中，发明专利授权量排名第2～10位的特定专业技术国内外有较大不同，如国内C02F9/00-9/14技术（水、废水或污水的多级处理）国内所获得的专利授权量排第二位，而在国外排名中排在第8位；C04B18/04-18/12（废物，废料）和B03D1/00-B03D1/26（浮选）技术的授权量在国内均进入前十名，而在国外的排名中却跌出前十的排位。这表明，在特定专利技术领域层面，我国节能环保产业国内外集中创新的技术领域不一致，国内外在各特定技术领域的竞争激烈。（3）虽然我国节能环保产业国内外在某些具体创新技术领域不一致，但产业总体的创新热点基本保持一致。我国节能环保产业要想在激烈的国际竞争中突围而出，就必须采取恰当的措施，激励发明创造，提高技术的核心竞争力，使节能环保技术逐渐缩小与国外先进技术水平的差距。

表4-3 2008～2013年节能环保技术发明专利国内外授权量特定专业技术分布 （件）

特定专业技术	国内		国外	
	授权量	排名	授权量	排名
C02F1/00-C02F1/78	7 049	1	1 042	1
C02F9/00-9/14	3 637	2	128	8
C02F3/00-3/34	3 537	3	284	4
B01D53/48-53/60	1 329	4	188	5
C02F11/00-11/20	1 312	5	149	6
B09B3/00	1 078	6	140	7
C04B18/04-18/12	649	7	27	16
F24F3/00-3/16	532	8	334	3
F24F1/00-1/04	462	9	563	2
B03D1/00-B03D1/26	453	10	52	12

（八）我国节能环保产业技术发明专利发展特点

节能环保技术是当前科技创新中最活跃的领域之一，节能环保技术的发展，必将引起全球科学技术的革新及经济结构和利益格局的重大调整。节能环保产业是中国加快培育和发展的七大战略性新兴产业之一，是中国改变经济发展模式，促进产业链升级改造的关键性产业。而发明专利的技术水平正是该产业发展成功与否的关键，同时专利技术的开发也是节能环保企业参与国内外市场竞争的重要战略内容。通过分析发现，我国节能环保产业发明专利分布的态势具有以下特点。

1. 节能环保产业技术创新能力明显增强

2010年，国务院确定将节能环保产业作为七大战略性新兴产业之首；2012年，国务院相继发布《"十二五"国家战略性新型产业规划》及《"十二五"节能环保产业发展规划》，详细指出了环保产业发展的重点领域、关键技术和具体路线等。这些政策措施的相继出台，为我国节能环保产业的发展奠定了良好的基础。在国家政策的有效指导下，节能环保技术创新活动更为活跃，各省市也相继出台一系列措施促进技术创新，鼓励发明创造，使得我国的节能环保技术呈跨越式发展，节能环保技术的专利申请量及所获的授权量逐年递增。节能环保技术专利申请量及授权量的大幅提高大大促进了我国节能环保产业的发展。目前，我国的环保产业已初具规模，某些环保产品或技术已达到国际领先水平，并在国际市场占据一定的市场地位。

2. 节能环保产业各子技术产业发展不均衡

在节能环保产业三大子技术产业中，节能产业与资源循环利用的创新能力均不强，产业各自的发展还有待深入发展。在我国节能环保产业中，环境治理子产业则得到良好的发展，专利授权量远多于其他两个子产业。这一方面说明环境治理领域是我国节能环保产业的热点投资研发领域，另一方面从某种意义上也说明我国环境问题突出，亟须有效的环境治理技术加强对环境污染的干预与治理。

3. 节能环保产业发明专利国内申请授权量地区分布严重不均衡

我国节能环保产业的地区发展严重不均衡。当前，我国节能环保产业的发明专利的申请和授权都集中在北京及东部沿海省市，北京、江苏、浙江、广东和上海五省市的发明专利授权量占国内授权总量的一半以上。节能环保产业发明专利申请授权地区分布不均，集中分布在东部发达省市，表明东部省市仍然是我国节能环保产业集中地，中、西部在该产业的竞争力明显不足。但随着国家政策的有效指导，中、西部在该产业呈较好的发展态势，如中部省份中，湖南和湖北对该产业的发展及竞争力逐渐增强，技术专利所获的授权量进入全国前十位。随着节能环保产业的深入发展，中、西部省市必将在该产业中拥有更强的竞争力。

4.节能产业技术创新领域主要集中于高效环保空调与热泵技术

我国节能产业主要技术领域的发明专利申请总体布局表明与人类工作生活密切相关的技术领域，发明创造活动更活跃，如节能产业中的高效环保空调与热泵技术，由于现在生活对空调的依赖性，对高效环保节能空调提出了更高的要求，因而在该技术领域的发明创造更活跃。而对一些与人类生活不直接相关的技术领域，由于参与人数、技术要求及使用范围等方面的限制，发明创造活动较弱，如节能产业中高效工业锅炉设计制造技术及余热余能利用技术。

5.资源循环利用产业主要集中于餐厨垃圾处理与综合利用等技术

我国资源循环利用产业中，与人类社会生活密切相关的餐厨垃圾处理与综合利用技术和城市污水污泥资源化技术发明创造活动活跃，发明专利所获得的授权量占该产业全部主要技术领域专利授权量的30%左右，分别列第一、第二位。废旧物质拆解分拣处理技术及再创造技术的发明力最薄弱，其中废旧物质拆解分拣处理技术仅占该产业专利授权总量的3.5%，再创造关键技术也仅占2.2%，专利所获的授权量位列最低。资源的再创造技术对资源的循环利用有效性有重要作用，而废旧物质拆解分拣处理技术有利于产业效率的提高，但我国资源循环利用产业中，再创造技术和分拣处理技术仍未能发挥出其在资源循环利用产业中应有的作用。与国外的专利授权情况相比，国内对煤矸石膏综合利用技术发明专利所获得的授权量仍占较大的比例，这表明我国对煤炭资源利用的依赖程度仍然较强，在该技术领域的创新活动较国外更加活跃。

6. 环境治理产业集中于高浓度有机废水控制技术

环境治理技术是我国节能环保产业的关键技术，其技术良好发展，直接影响我国节能环保产业在国际竞争中站稳阵脚，赢得竞争的先机。我国环境治理子产业各大技术领域的发展严重不均衡，高浓度有机废水的控制技术成为该产业高度集中的技术领域。重金属废水、废气、废渣污染控制技术，重金属、持久有机污染物污染土壤恢复技术及烟气脱硫脱硝关键技术等未能得到有效的发展，需要政府提供更多政策指引，更好地引导该产业均衡良好地发展。

7. 国内外节能环保产业发明专利授权量布局总体一致

国内外节能环保产业研究发展的热点均集中在环境治理这一领域，该领域发明专利的授权量远高于节能和资源循环利用这两个领域。环境治理领域成为国内外节能环保产业研发的重点，说明全球环境破坏严重，致使各国不得不投入更大的精力和更多的金钱去治理已被严重污染的环境。但节能和资源循环利用领域侧重于环境污染的预防，这两个领域的产业如果发展良好，将大大减少人类对环境污染治理的资源投入，极大地促进环保事业的发展。目前，我国的节能环保产业中的节能和资源循环利用领域仍有待深入发展。而在特定技术领域，C02F1/00—C02F1/78（水、废水或污水的处理技术）的发明专利无论是国内申请或国外所获得的专利授权均以绝对的优势领先于其他技术领域。虽然排名前十位的特定技术领域中，国内与国外排名有所变化，但总体上，国内外在节能环保产业技术重点创新及研究热点领域基本保持一致。这表明，国外节能环保技术强国的核心专利技术将极大影响我国节能环保产业的发展。如果国内的创新主体在这些热点研究领域未能有所突破，或未能掌握产业的核心技术，我国的节能环保产业将在激烈的国际市场竞争处于不利的地位。因此，我们必须采取恰当的措施，激励发明创造，提高技术的核心竞争力，使节能环保技术创新能力走在全球的前列。

（九）专利及其制度对发展节能环保产业技术方面存在的问题

我国节能环保产业产生于20世纪70年代，经过40多年的发展，我国环保产业已初具规模，某些环保产品或技术已达到国际领先水平。近年来，国家出台的一系列政策措施为我国节能环保产业保驾护航，消除该产业发展的政策障碍，使得该产业发展迅猛，相关技术水平也得到大幅提高。虽然我国节能环保技术发展态势良好，但技术水平仍然不高，产业技术发展仍存在不少亟须解决的问题。

1. 节能环保产业授权发明专利创造方面存在的问题

（1）节能环保产业技术授权发明专利数量较大但质量普遍不高。2008～2013年，国家知识产权局授予节能环保技术发明专利共27 327件，数额较大，但专利质量普遍不高，专利的市场化程度不高。自2010年国家将节能环保产业列为战略性新型产业，加大对该产业发展的扶持力度，国家知识产权局对该产业技术发明的授权量也明显增多，但专利授权量的数额变化与产业的发展状况并不匹配。目前，我国节能环保产业发展仍未成熟，对产业技术应用仍然处在低水平的模仿应用阶段，而产业技术发明专利并未能为企业的发展提供良好的核心技术。现阶段我国节能环保技术授权发明专利中，有相当一部分的专利技术往往只是处在实验室阶段，还不适合市场的产业化，因而对节能环保产业发展的推动力有限。

（2）节能环保产业技术授权发明专利所属区域及技术领域分布严重不均。我国节能环保产业的专利授权量集中分布于东部沿海发达省市，中、西部技术创新力量薄弱。在技术领域的分布中，授权发明专利中，绝大多数发明专利集中于环境治理子产业领域，节能及资源循环利用技术方面的授权发明专利相对较少，其专利技术创新能力远不如环境治理子产业。在各子产业发展中，技术创新力量均以较大的比例集中于一个或两个技术领域。节能环保产业的区域及技术领域的授权专利布局的严重不均衡，将不利于我国节能环保产业的深入发展。

（3）节能环保产业创新主体专利战略乃至专利意识较弱。我国节能环保产业中，中小企业对技术专利的认识不足，缺乏自主创新的动力，即使掌握产业核心技术，往往又对知识产权缺乏必要的认识，使企业自身的核心技术力量得不到有效的保护，从而错失发展的良机。

2. 专利审查程序对促进节能环保产业发展发明存在的问题

2012年，国家知识产权局明确对节能环保等战略性新兴产业的发明专利申请实行优先审查制度，这一措施将有助于进一步加快节能环保产业重要科技成果的转化，大大促进产业的发展。但是在国家知识产权局的优先审查制度中并未建立相应的具体适用优先审查制度的配套措施。如国家知识产权局只是笼统地说明节能环保产业适用优先审查制度，但没有明确何种标准可以称为节能环保技术，节能环保的标准如何判断，哪些具体技术属于优先审查的范围等相关问题。而优先审查制度本身也容易导致专利审查人员对申请专利的新颖性、创造性及实用性的错误判断，从而使一些简单模仿专利技术的专利申请顺利通过专利审查程序获得专利权，容易造成市场应用的混乱及低效率，不利于节能环保产业的可持续发展。

3. 专利授权标准对促进节能环保产业发展发明存在的问题

专利授权标准是影响节能环保产业发展的关键因素之一，其中创造性标准的把握最为关键。创造性要件是专利制度的最后守门员和可专利性的终极要件。它是专利法的核心概念，是可专利性的试金石，体现了专利制度的有限保护与专利权人公开发明技术方案的平衡。❶随着专利制度对技术进步推动力的增强，保护客体的不断拓展，创造性对专利制度功能的适度发挥越来越重

---

❶ R. Polk Wagner, Katherine J. Strandburg. "The Obviousness Requirement in the Patent Law", *University of Pennsylvania Law Review*, Vol. 155: 96.

要。❶ 司法实践中，不管是国内还是国外，绝大多数专利侵权案件都会被提出专利无效的反诉。而专利无效的反诉指控中，创造性不足或不具创造性是侵权人指控的最主要武器。在特定时间，发明对本领域普通技术人员而言是否显而易见是发明可专利性的基础，也是每件专利讨价还价的核心。❷ 而发明是否显而易见是一种抽象的价值判断，易于主观化。在实务上，至今未能发展出具体、统一适用于不同案例的判断标准，难免会因为判断者的科技素养及训练不同而导致其判断专利创造性的结果有所不同。❸ 和其他战略性新兴产业发明创造一样，节能环保产业技术授权专利标准的把握非常重要。为了快速发展我国节能环保产业等战略性新兴产业，在把握专利授权标准，尤其是创造性标准时，如何掌握创造性标准的高度，不同战略性新兴产业授权专利的创造性标准是否需要区分，如果需要，如何区分等问题均需要进一步探讨，以便发挥专利制度对战略性新兴产业的促进作用。

---

❶ John F Duffy. "KSR v. Teleflex: Predictable Reform of Patent Substance and Procedure in the Judiciary". in http://www.michiganlawreview.org/firstimpressions/vol106/duffy.pdf.

❷ Lee Petherbridge, R Polk Wagner. "The Federal Circuit and Patentability: An Empirical Assessment of the Law of Obviousness", in *Texas Law Review*; Jun 2007; (85): 7.

❸ 董安丹："美国专利法上之非显著性——历史发展及GRAHAM原则（上）"，载《智慧财产权》1999年第10期，第80～87页。

4. 专利维持制度在促进战略性新兴产业发展方面存在的问题

鉴于绝大多数国家和地区的专利法规定专利权人为了使其专利有效必须交纳年费，所以关于专利维持的数据资料和年费交纳情况就包含专利质量分布的信息。因此，通过从发明专利未缴专利年费而被终止这一现象反推专利质量，即在其他条件不变的情况下，专利维持时间与专利质量成正相关，专利维持时间越短，专利质量越低，反之专利质量越高。从经济学理论的理性经济人假设出发，一个理性经济人在交纳年费维持发明专利时，必须权衡维持该发明专利的成本与收益。对个人而言，收益的多少直接体现了专利质量高低。❶ 专利维持年费制度是专利维持制度的核心制度。专利维持费是指为了维持专利继续有效而依据专利法规定向专利行政机构定期缴纳的费用。专利维持年费制度是指通过要求专利权人缴纳专利维持年费，适度增加专利维持成本，影响专利维持时间，平衡专利权人和社会公众利益，促进技术创新的制度。专利权人是否维持专利，维持专利多长时间主要取决于其权衡维持专利成本和收益的结果。专利获得授权后，维持成本主要是交纳年费，专利维持

---

❶ 乔永忠、朱雪忠："基于维持时间的发明专利质量实证研究——以1994年中国专利局授权发明专利为例"，见《优秀专利调查研究报告集（六）》，知识产权出版社2010年版，第291~311页。

年费的多少和不同档次之间增加数额幅度的大小会对专利的维持时间产生非常重要的影响。因此，专利维持年费的多少将直接影响专利维持时间的长短，即专利维持年费制度的合适程度将直接影响专利维持时间的合理分布。❶ 我国专利维持费标准存在一定问题，如维持年费长时间很少发生变化，现在沿用2008年标准，目前人民币购买力与2008年相比，已经发生很大变化，所以对技术创新的促进作用也发生了变化；又如维持年费数额与权力要求数无关等。为了促进节能环保等战略性新兴产业的发展，是否在专利维持费方面给予适度政策倾斜，需要进一步研究。

5. 其他相关法律及政策在促进战略性新兴产业发展方面存在的问题

虽然我国的节能环保产业已有30多年的发展历史，但由于产业发展前期的不重视，且节能环保产业本身涉及的面又很广，与产业相关的法律法规还不够健全，节能环保产业的市场环境还没有发展成熟。有效的法律法规运行是产业稳定良好发展的基础。目前，与节能环保产业相关的法律法规包括《中华人民共和国环境保护法》《中华人民共和国环境影响评价法》以及指导节

---

❶ 乔永忠："专利维持时间影响因素研究"，载《科研管理》2011年第7期，第143～152页。

能环保产业发展宏观规划《"十二五"节能环保产业发展规划》。虽然与环境保护有关的法律体系已经初步形成，但直接应用与节能环保产业的法律法规仍然欠缺，相关法律法规仍然跟不上产业发展的需求。

（十）小　结

节能环保产业是我国加快培育和发展的七大战略性新兴产业之一，是我国改变经济发展模式，促进产业链升级改造的关键性产业。❶而发明专利的技术水平正是该产业发展成功与否的关键，同时专利技术的开发也是节能环保企业参与国内外市场竞争的重要战略内容。通过对我国节能环保产业发明专利分布的态势分析，可以得出如下六点结论：（1）我国节能环保产业逐渐进入平稳发展阶段；（2）我国节能环保产业发展较快，但各子产业发展不均衡，环境治理产业的技术创新活动最活跃；（3）我国节能产业的技术创新领域主要集中于高效环保空调与热泵技术，资源循环产业主要集中于餐厨垃圾处理与综合利用技术和城市污水污泥资源化技术，环境治理产业则高度集中于高浓度有机废水的控制技术；（4）我国节能环保产业中，各相关技术的国内外专利布

---

❶　张延平、汤萱："战略性新兴产业发展理论分析与实践经验借鉴——以广东省节能环保产业为例"，载《现代城市研究》2012年第7期，第81～87页。

局总体保持一致；（5）企业是我国节能环保产业最核心的技术创新主体，个人和大专院校在该产业的发明创造活动也较活跃，科研单位和机关团体则较薄弱；（6）国内外节能环保产业研发重点基本一致，发明专利的申请授权量在各重点战略领域中分布不均衡，其中环境治理领域的专利申请量最大，而特定技术领域中，我国节能环保产业发明专利又集中在"水、废水或污水的处理"这一特定技术领域。

五、我国战略性新兴产业发明专利布局及问题*
——以新能源汽车产业中奇瑞、比亚迪、长安和吉利为例

新能源汽车是指采用非常规车用燃料作为动力来源或使用常规车用燃料、采用新型车载动力装置，综合车辆动力控制和驱动方面的先进技术，形成技术原理先进，具有新技术、新结构的汽车。新能源汽车产业是指从事新能源汽车生产与运用的行业，是中国七大战略性新兴产业之一。新能源汽车产业的特性至少包括以下五个方面：（1）战略性。发展新能源汽车，不是因为缺乏石油，或者现在买不到石油，或者世界上没有石油；也不是因为电力供应过剩，没有地方用，汽车业必须考虑战略性发展，要寻求最广阔的能源持续提供的可能性。（2）先进性，即创新性。新能源汽车在很多方面都有待原始创新，不只是现有汽车的简单升级。对这种先进性和替代效应，新能源汽车发展不是简单地替代过去，而

---

* 本部分内容由乔永忠和张恬恬共同创作完成。

是技术创新和跨越，所以必须保证先进性。（3）系统性。新能源汽车产业界不能按照过去传统汽车行业的思路，单独完成新能源汽车整体产业的发展，还要带动相关产品和产业形成新的产业链，如过去汽车上的电池就是蓄电池，只需完成简单的功能如启动、照明等，现在搭载的电池属于动力电池，还有电子控制系统。一定要系统考虑，协同创新才能推动产业发展。（4）市场性。新能源汽车必须遵循国家的技术创新基本方针或者基本框架，要坚持市场化。（5）多元性。在相当一段时间内，对于替代燃料汽车，无论是混合动力汽车、纯电池驱动汽车，还是燃料电池汽车，每一个企业都可以根据自己在市场中的定位，结合自己的能力，在不同的发展阶段推出不同产品，因为这是一个多样性的市场、多元技术并存的市场。❶

近年来，全球汽车产业受到金融危机的影响陷入全球性衰退的泥淖，另外，迫于资源、环境的压力，哥本哈根会议之后，世界各国达成共识，要求进一步减少对石油资源的依赖，降低二氧化碳排放，这也就成为世界各国汽车产业未来发展的必然选择。美、日、欧等国家或者地区均开始强势推行新能源汽车的战略部署，以电

---

❶ 张小虞："发展电动汽车信念不可动摇"，载中国城市低碳经济网http://www.cusdn.org.cn/news_detail.php?id=227309, 2014-06-21。

动车作为重点发展目标，加大研发与资金投入力度，力争抢占汽车行业未来竞争的优势地位。我国新能源汽车产业经过十多年的发展，已经拥有一批自主创新成果，积累了一定的技术集成能力，产业布局初具规模，但在国家补贴政策的刺激下，我国新能源汽车产业出现的发展态势存在一定风险。一方面，多家自主研发企业在新能源汽车领域所拥有的核心专利技术是否存在知识产权风险还有待进一步核实。另一方面，目前电动汽车产业的配套企业，虽技术比较先进，但规模普遍较小，在没有规模化生产的情况下，商业化启动阶段必然成本高。实际上，我国新能源汽车产业中，不少企业是在做"面子工程"，真正投入新能源技术的研发费用有限，很多企业依然还是等待引进技术，而无自己的核心技术。专利技术的科学布局可以在保证企业整体先进技术发展的前提下把握自身优势，开拓创新，争取在新能源汽车相关专利技术中有所突破。比较分析相关技术领域典型公司的专利布局，可以为我国相关产业发展提供参考。因此，研究该领域专利布局对我国新能源汽车产业技术创新和发展具有重要意义。

我国战略性新兴产业中大型企业技术水平相对较高、创新能力较强，不同产业的技术水平与国外的差距同样存在异质性。❶ 因此，本研究报告以我国新能源汽车产业中的奇瑞汽车股份有限公司（以下简称"奇瑞"）、比亚迪股份有限公司（以下简称"比亚迪"）、浙江吉利控股集团有限公司（以下简称"吉利"）以及长安汽车股份有限公司（以下简称"长安"）四大重要企业为例，结合企业发展战略，分析其新能源汽车产业专利布局，以揭示中国新能源汽车产业专利布局特点及存在问题，并为我国的新能源汽车产业的发展与投资提供理论参考。

（一）新能源汽车产业及其专利布局研究现状

2013年新能源汽车实现快速增长，但对于汽车产业总体的影响仍很有限。据汽车工业协会统计，全年新能源汽车销售量在1.76万辆左右，增长37.9%，其中纯电动销售14 604辆，插电式混合动力销售3 038辆，分别比上年增长28.4%和114.5%。但相较于全国2 198.4万辆的汽车总销量，新能源汽车销量比重尚不足1‰。❷

2012年新能源汽车产业授权数量前十位的省市，

---

❶ 邢红萍、卫平："我国战略性新兴产业企业技术创新特征分析——基于全国七省市战略性新兴产业企业问卷调查"，载《中国科技论坛》2013 年第7期，第66～73页。

❷ 国家信息中心信息资源开发部："战略性新兴产业2013年发展形势及2014年展望"，载http://www.sic.gov.cn/News/82/2591.htm, 2014-05-31。

包括广东、北京、江苏、上海、安徽、浙江、重庆、湖南、山东和湖北，排在前十的省市发明专利授权总量为793件，同比增长53.4%。相比2011年，各省市授权量均有所上升，特别是广东，从2011年的63件增至2012年的124件，增幅为96.8%，取代安徽跃居第一，且高出第二位北京40件，而安徽则退居第五，江苏排在北京之后，从原来的第五位升至第三位，授权量仅比北京少一件。湖南挤入前十，而辽宁则退出前十排位。从2011年、2012年总体来看，广东的综合实力最强，获得授权最多，北京次之，安徽排在第三位，江苏、上海和浙江实力也不容小觑。❶

比较分析相关技术领域典型公司的专利布局，可以为我国相关产业发展提供重要参考。❷ 现有研究多集中在新能源产业及新能源汽车产业整体布局的政策分析及发展策略方面。如研究显示，美国将研究中心放在氢动力燃料电池车，日本则推崇混合动力汽车；❸ 制约中国新能源汽车产业化发展的最大难题是电池造价贵、容量

---

❶ 国家知识产权局规划发展司："战略性新兴产业授权发明专利统计报告"，载《专利统计简报》2013年第11期，第38～39页。

❷ 栾春娟、王续琨、刘则渊："三星电子公司与华为技术公司专利布局的比较"，载《科学管理研究》2008年第2期，第117～121页。

❸ 杨海霞："新能源汽车的中国机遇"，载《中国投资》2008年9月11日。

低、不稳定等问题；❶ 我国新能源汽车发展存在技术创新能力低，基础设施不完善等问题；❷ 中国必须绕开发达国家设置的技术壁垒，加强技术开发，推动新能源汽车发展的同时兼顾传统汽车技术升级。❸ 新能源产业专利问题研究成果主要有以下几个方面：统计分析新能源汽车领域的专利类型、申请主体及关键技术领域；❹ 比较研究中日新能源汽车产业授权专利；❺ 探讨中国新能源汽车产业专利标准化问题；❻ 提出我国新能源技术领域自主品牌汽车企业专利布局问题；❼ 比较研究中国和日、美等发达国家在新能源汽车涵盖的主要车型和关键技术专利态势。❽ 另外，广东省已经发布《新能源汽车产业专利分析与预警报告》，2009～2013年，广东省在

---

❶ 袁华智、寒小平、袁华剑："我国新能源汽车产业竞争力研究"，载《科技管理研究》2012年第17期，第42页。

❷ Chen Liuqin:"China's New Energy Vehicle Industry: Problems and Challenges". *in Electricity*, 2012,2.

❸ 李文辉、孙晨光："实现新能源汽车跨越式发展的可能性和路径选择"，载《中国商界》2010年第12期，第372～373页。

❹ 徐国祥、余碧涛、李福燊、艾娟："我国新能源汽车领域专利申请情况分析"，载《电池》2012年第5期，第289～292页。

❺ 郑薇："新能源汽车的技术专利研究"，载《汽车技术》2009年第5期，第43～45页。

❻ 李薇薇："新能源汽车产业的专利标准化战略制定与实施"，载《中国科技论坛》2012年第6期，第62～68页。

❼ 王永、汪张林："自主品牌汽车企业新能源专利分析"，载《汽车工程师》2011年第4期，第19～21页。

❽ 国家知识产权局规划发展司："新能源汽车产业专利态势分析报告"，载《专利统计简报》2011年第11期，第1～16页。

新能源汽车领域专利在纯电动汽车、插电式混合动力汽车、燃料电池汽车、锂电子动力电池、驱动电机、整车控制等主要领域中，专利申请量均位居全国前列。❶江苏省常州市发布了《新能源车辆行业专利预警分析》。❷重要企业是产业发展的支柱，但对我国新能源汽车重要企业关键技术领域的专利布局及发展态势报道不多。

（二）研究对象与数据收集

1. 研究对象

（1）技术领域。新能源汽车包括混合动力汽车（HEV）、纯电动汽车（BEV，包括太阳能汽车）、燃料电池电动汽车（FCEV）、氢发动机汽车、其他新能源（如高效储能器、二甲醚）汽车等各类别产品。我国现阶段重点发展的技术方向主要为混合动力汽车、纯电动汽车与燃料电池车。

（2）重点企业。我国国内专利申请量混合动力汽车领域前三的企业是奇瑞、比亚迪和长安；纯电动汽车领域前三的企业是比亚迪、奇瑞、清华；燃料电池汽车领

---

❶ "广东新能源汽车领域专利申请量位居全国第一"，载http://www.sipo.gov.cn/mtjj/2014/201406/t20140604_959930.html，2014-06-05。

❷ "江苏常州发布新能源车辆行业专利预警分析报告"，载http://www.chinairn.com/news/20130330/114543203.html，2013-12-02。

域前三的企业是清华、上海神力、上海燃料电池汽车；动力电池技术领域申请量排名前三的企业是比亚迪、奇瑞、天津力神。❶ 因此，本研究报告拟重点研究奇瑞、比亚迪、吉利和长安公司的专利布局特点及问题。

2. 数据检索

本研究报告的所有专利数据均从SooPat专利数据库（http://www2.soopat.com/Home/IIndex）检索，检索方式为"申请主体+IPC分类号"，时间区间为2008～2013年，对奇瑞、比亚迪、吉利和长安四家企业专利授权量进行统计。❷

（三）数据分析

由于在发展战略性新兴产业过程中，首要任务是发掘具有引领带动作用并且能够实现突破的若干重点技术方向，所以企业的专利组合状况通常很好地体现了所属企业的专利布局策略。所谓专利组合，是指某一机构所拥有的共有某项关键技术特征的专利集合，简单来说可以理解为由某一技术领域内上、中、下游专利组合而成的能够有效阻击竞争对手、占领该技术领域和产品市

---

❶ 国家知识产权局规划发展司：《新能源汽车产业专利态势分析报告》2011年第18期。

❷ 不同重要领域的个别IPC分类号可能存在重复，对重复数据采取人工统计。

场的一个专利集，其目的是保护组织内的核心专利以巩固核心技术。由此可见，通过分析某一企业的专利组合状况能够很好地看出该企业专利技术的布局，掌握其核心技术，并针对薄弱环节进行新技术的研发与突破。通常，专利组合是通过绘制专利地图来体现的，通过对相关技术变量的分析与收集，借助相关软件，以图谱的方式对专利组合情况进行系统的分析。但是，在收集相关数据的时候我们可以发现，由于绘制专利地图所需要的相关数据和信息，如专利市场吸引率、关键发明人数量等属于企业内部信息，收集难度大，且绘图软件操作复杂，国内尚无相关软件等因素，最终放弃了通过专利地图体现专利布局的方式，而选择采用通过分析不同企业在核心技术领域内获得的专利授权数量来体现不同企业的专利布局状况的方式。

最终，通过数据收集，对奇瑞、比亚迪、吉利和长安四家企业在混合动力汽车、纯电动汽车、燃料电池汽车和动力电池技术四大领域内关键核心技术上的专利布局进行了阐述与分析。

1. 四大技术领域专利整体布局

图5-1分析了2008～2013年四大技术领域的整体专利布局，可以看出：在混合动力汽车领域，奇瑞、比亚迪、吉利授权专利持平，长安授权专利弱势地位明显；

纯电动汽车领域，各企业授权专利数量总体相差不大，两极化现象不明显。总体专利授权量最低的是燃料电池汽车领域，奇瑞、吉利与长安只有少量授权专利。四家企业在电池技术领域授权专利优势明显，特别是比亚迪总量达到723件，超过其他三家企业的总和。

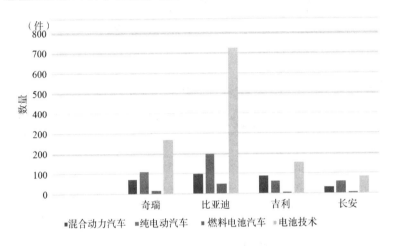

图5-1 四大技术领域专利整体布局

具体而言，四家企业在四个主要技术领域分布呈现以下四个特征：（1）比亚迪专利授权量在四大技术领域中最多，在电池技术领域的授权专利取得绝对优势；（2）混合动力汽车领域长安落后于其他三家企业，说明其在该领域技术创新水平相对落后；（3）吉利在纯电动汽车领域的专利授权量低于混合动力汽车领域，专利布局侧重有所不同；（4）从专利授权总量来看，长安专利授权量总体偏低，虽然电池技术领域专利授权量相对其他技术领域较多。说明四家企业对不同的技术领域侧重点是各不相同的。

2. 混合动力汽车技术领域专利布局

混合动力汽车是指车上装有两个以上动力源（蓄电池、燃料电池、太阳能电池、内燃机车）发电机组汽车。在由传统汽车向理想新能源的过渡过程中，混合动力是企业研发的必由之路。四家企业在混合动力汽车技术领域的专利布局如表5-1所示。

表5-1　混合动力汽车技术专利布局　　　　　（件）

	奇瑞	比亚迪	吉利	长安
原动机布置或安装（B60K6）	14+0	38+16	35+18	5+2
车辆控制系统（B60W20）	15+0	21+1	4+3	8+0
电源电力牵引（B60L11）	13+1	4+6	9+4	2+1
车辆子系统联合控制（B60W10）	24+2	8+0	7+5	8+2
总计	69	94	85	28

注：表内数据格式为：发明专利授权量+实用新型专利授权量，下同。

对混合动力汽车技术领域内的专利布局进行概括与分析得到该领域所采用的核心技术分别是：原动机布置或安装（IPC专利分类号为B60K6，下同）、车辆控制系统（B60W20）、电源电力牵引（B60L11）、车辆子系统联合控制（B60W10）。四企业在混合动力汽车具体技术领域具有以下特征。（1）在原动机布置或安装技术领域，比亚迪和吉利拥有专利授权量都具有优势，奇瑞和长安专利授权数量较少；车辆控制系统技术领域比亚迪专利较多，优势地位明显，奇瑞、吉利和长安专利很少；电源电力牵引技术领域长安拥有的专利数量较少；车辆子系统联合控制技术领域奇瑞专利授权量接近其他三家企业的总和，其中比亚迪的专利授权数量仅为个位数。（2）在奇瑞企业内部，各技术领域内的专利授权数量较为均衡，在车辆子系统联合控制技术领域授权专利优势明显；比亚迪和吉利都是在原动机布置或安装技术领域具有绝对的优势，比本企业其他技术领域专利授权总量还多；长安专利授权量相对较少，多个技术领域都只有少数授权专利。（3）在混合动力汽车领域，各技术领域内的发明专利授权量都远远高于实用新型专利授权量，说明各企业在技术创新中的成果较为显著，专利质量较高。可见，各企业在混合动力汽车领域的专利授权量较大，奇瑞、比亚迪和吉利的总量相差不大，但长安授权专利数量较少。在该技术领域，各企业的专利以发明专利为主，实用新型专利比例比较低。

3.纯电动汽车技术领域专利布局

2008～2013年四企业在纯电动汽车技术的专利授

权量布局如表5-2所示。根据表5-2可知，在纯电动汽车领域，比亚迪专利授权量最多，奇瑞次之，竞争优势明显；吉利和长安专利授权量较为接近，总数较少。

表5-2 纯电动汽车技术专利布局　　　（件）

	奇瑞	比亚迪	吉利	长安
电源电力牵引（B60L11）	13+3	3+2	2+0	0
电池组充电/供电装置（H02J7）	46+14	58+81	14+20	14+3
电池及其制造（H01M10）	8+0	10+16	2+5	7+4
结构零件或制造方法（H01M2）	4+3	4+6	1+9	4+10
车辆传动装置布置/安装（B60K17）	8+7	4+15	0+7	4+9
合计	106	198	60	55

对纯电动汽车技术领域内的专利布局进行概括与分析得到该领域所采用的核心技术分别是：电源电力牵引（B60L11）、电池组充电/供电装置（H02J7）、电池及其制造（H01M10）、结构零件或制造方法（H01M2）、车辆传动装置布置/安装（B60K17）。通过分析，可以发现四企业在主要技术领域专利分布呈如下四个特征。（1）电源电力牵引技术领域奇瑞专利授权量较多，比亚迪和吉利只有个位授权专利，长安没有授权专利。结合专利整体布局发现，电源电力牵引技术领域不仅涉及

纯电动汽车技术领域，同时属于混合动力汽车领域和燃料电池汽车领域的核心技术，说明新能源汽车产业各技术领域间存在一定的交叉与联系。（2）电池组充电/供电装置技术领域四企业专利技术最为集中，其中比亚迪优势尤其明显，专利授权量达到139件，但60%以上为实用新型专利，发明专利比例较低。（3）在电池及其制造、结构零件或制造方法、车辆传动装置的布置/安装技术领域，四企业授权专利分布较为均匀，比亚迪微弱领先。值得注意的是，整体专利授权量偏低的长安，在这三个技术领域显出较为强劲的竞争力。（4）奇瑞发明专利授权量远高于实用新型专利授权量，而比亚迪、吉利和长安实用新型专利授权量比重更大，说明奇瑞在发展中虽然专利数量落后于比亚迪，但更加注重专利质量的发展。

总之，纯电动汽车领域内各企业发展较为均衡，整体优势较为突出，专利授权量差距极端化不明显，比亚迪处于领先地位，但奇瑞发明专利授权量比重更大，专利质量较高。

4. 燃料电池汽车技术领域专利布局

对燃料电池汽车技术领域内的专利布局进行概括与分析（见表5-3）所得所采用的核心技术分别是：燃料电池及其制造（H01M8）、电极件（H01M4）、电源电力牵引（B60L11）、直流功率输入变换为输出（H02M3）。可以发现四家企业在燃料电池汽车技术领域分布呈现如下特征。（1）电极件和电源电力牵引技术领域专利授权量基本为零。电极件技术领域多为磷酸铁锂子电池相关专利，与燃料电池关联性不大。电源电力牵引技术也是混合动力汽车和纯电动汽车核心技术，该领域燃料电池相关专利为零。（2）燃料电池汽车技术领域，授权专利集中于燃料电池及其制造和直流功率输入变换为输出两项技术，其中比亚迪居领先地位，且发明专利比例高，技术含量高。可见，燃料电池汽车领域专利授权量总体偏低，处于四大技术领域最后一位，专利分布不均，极端化现象明显，技术创新有待加强，是企业技术研发的重点。由于燃料电池电动车能够实现行驶过程中二氧化碳的零排放，而且具备续航里程长、燃料加注时间短等优势，因此它将是汽车未来发展的终极方向。但燃料电池汽车领域技术创新并不明显。四家企业在燃料电池领域专利授权量状况如上所述。比亚迪专利授权数量最多，其次是奇瑞，吉利和长安专利授权量很少，说明四企业在该领域专利技术差异性较大，技术水平分化严重。有两种原因导致这一现象出现：（1）比亚迪前身是一家电池生产企业，拥有中国最早的电池技术专利，其在电动汽车领域具有绝对优势；（2）比亚迪设立了中央研究院、电子研究院、汽车工程研究院以及电力科学研究院，负责高科技产品和技术研发。

表5-3 燃料电池汽车技术专利布局 （件）

	奇瑞	比亚迪	吉利	长安
燃料电池及其制造（H01M8）	0	17+4	2+0	1+0
电极件（H01M4）	1+0	0	0	0
电源电力牵引（B60L11）	0	0	0	0
直流功率输入变换为输出（H02M3）	8+3	13+11	0	0+1
合计	14	44	2	3

5. 电池技术领域的专利布局

对动力电池技术领域内的专利布局的概括与分析（见表5-4）所得该领域采用的核心技术分别是：电池及其制造（H01M10）、结构零件或制造方法（H01M2）、电极件（H01M4）、电路或流体管路及其原件布置（B60R16）、电动力装置的布置或安装（B60K1）。从四企业在电池技术领域授权专利布局可以发现，四企业都比较重视电池技术领域专利布局，专利授权量都占企业专利授权量比例较高。这是因为以电力取代燃油是用新能源汽车取代燃油动力汽车的关键。因此，不论混合动力汽车、纯电动汽车、燃料电池汽车都属于采用电能作为主要动力源的新能源汽车，电池技术就必然成为各企业重点研发的对象。根据数据，在电池技术领域，比亚迪专利授权量远超出其他三家企业专利授权量的总和。电池及其制造、结构零件或制造方法、电极件技术领域专利授权量具有明显优势，结构零件或制造方法实用新型专利为主，电极件技术发明专利占绝大多数，说明其专利分布侧重点各有不同，电极件技术的专利质量更高；在电路或流体管路及其原件布置和电动力装置的布置或安装技术领域，比亚迪专利授权量相对较低，且以实用新型专利为主，说明比亚迪在这两个技术领域没有优势。奇瑞各重点技术领域授权专利分布较为均匀。虽然结构零件或制造方法和电动力装置布置或安装技术领域专利授权量相对较低，但差距不大，且以发明专利较多。吉利与长安在该技术领域专利授权量较低，专利布局具有明显特征：（1）电池及其制造、结构零件或制造方法、电极件技术内授权量很少，电极件技术为零；（2）电路或流体管路及其原件布置和电动力装置布置或安装领域专利授权量相对较高，但是以实用新型为主，质量不高。可见，电池技术领域内各企业整体授权量较高，是专利布局的重点领域，但是各企业布局侧重点各不相同，差距较大。专利技术以实用新型为主，质量不高，突破不大。

表5-4 电池技术专利布局				（件）
	奇瑞	比亚迪	吉利	长安
电池及其制造（H01M10）	44+4	143+102	1+7	7+6
结构零件或制造方法（H01M2）	22+12	71+129	0+5	6+3
电极件（H01M4）	62+1	206+15	0	0
电路或流体管路及其原件布置（B60R16）	61+25	5+25	34+83	13+29
电动力装置的布置或安装（B60K1）	15+18	3+24	4+18	4+13
合计	265	723	152	81

　　总体来看，本部分通过对新能源汽车产业奇瑞、比亚迪、吉利和长安四家企业重点技术领域授权专利布局分析，得出如下结论：混合动力领域，奇瑞、比亚迪、吉利专利授权量相差不大，整体专利质量较高，长安授权专利技术水平较低；纯电动汽车领域，各企业发展较为均衡，整体优势较为突出，专利授权量差距极端化不明显，比亚迪处于领先地位，但奇瑞以质量取胜；燃料电池汽车领域，专利授权量总体偏低，专利分布不均，极端化现象明显；在电池技术领域，整体授权量较高，是专利布局的重点领域，但各企业专利布局差距明显。

（四）新能源汽车产业专利布局存在的问题

　　我国新能源汽车产业在发展中仍然存在一些问题，

结合权利要求书、保护范围和专利申请主体相关性等方面来看，这些问题的出现也并非偶然。

1. 基于专利申请主题的我国新能源汽车产业研发布局问题

我国新能源汽车产业研发的整体布局为"三纵三横"。"三纵"指的是混合动力汽车、纯电动汽车和燃料电池汽车，"三横"指的是多能源动力总成控制、驱动电机和动力蓄电池，其中"三横"是基础，"三横"中又以动力蓄电池为重点。❶结合研究报告分析结果，以四家企业在混合动力领域、纯电动汽车领域、燃料电池汽车领域和电池技术领域所取得专利成果作为研究对象，并发现其存在的一些问题，是符合我国现阶段发展重点国情的。研究发现，燃料电池汽车领域总体专利授权量较低，说明新能源汽车产业在燃料电池汽车领域的技术力量比较薄弱。燃料电池汽车主要以氢、太阳能等清洁能源为动力，是新能源汽车发展的目标，却处在发展的末端，究其原因与企业发展策略失衡和世界环境的影响是脱不开关系的。（1）燃料电池汽车不耗油也无须充电，不污染环境，是世界清洁能源汽车的较好选择，

---

❶ "中国新能源汽车十年路 '三纵三横'书发展路线"，载《科技日报》2012年11月19日，http://finance.chinanews.com/ny/2012/11-19/4338633.shtml，2014-06-16。

但这一技术在世界各国都尚未达到可以量产的水平，目前还处在研究开发和示范运行阶段。氢的制取、氢的储存、加氢站的建设和续驶里程是燃料电池汽车实现产业化需要解决的问题。因此，在世界大环境的影响下，我国燃料电池汽车发展缓慢，专利成果较少也就成为一种必然的现象。（2）由于与纯电动汽车和燃料电池汽车相比，混合动力汽车不需要建设配套的基础设施，技术复杂程度也相对较低，因而是新能源汽车可行性最高的发展方向，所以各企业都将技术投入到混合动力汽车领域和纯电动汽车领域，从而导致这两个领域的专利成果较多，自然成为布局的重中之重，忽略了燃料电池汽车领域的技术开发与布局。（3）通过前面的阐述，燃料电池汽车领域中电极件技术领域多为磷酸铁锂子电池相关专利，与燃料电池关联性不大。可见，我国新能源汽车产业重要企业的专利申请主题存在相当的方向性问题，而这些专利申请主题的方向性问题与企业技术研发的重点是分不开的。

2. 基于保护范围的我国新能源汽车产业的专利申请结构问题

我国新能源汽车产业授权专利结构不合理，核心技术不多。从技术开发力度来看，新能源汽车产业的专利授权实用新型专利占据最大比例，虽然在混合动力汽车技术领域和燃料电池汽车技术领域内，发明专利的比例更大，但是整体来看，实用新型专利仍是企业专利技术的主力军。发明是指对产品、方法或者其改进所提出的新的技术方案；实用新型，是指对产品的形状、构造或者其结合所提出的适于实用的新的技术方案。❶ 可见，发明专利可以保护产品、生产产品的方法以及产品的生产设备和产品用途，而实用新型专利则不能保护产品的生产方法和产品用途，因此在保护范围方面存在很大差异。由此可以说明，我国新能源汽车产业拥有的专利结构（发明专利与实用新型专利的比例）不够合理会在一定程度上造成该产业专利技术保护范围的不足。也可以看出，我国新能源汽车产业企业现阶段的技术研发投入和技术创新以及专利布局方面存在的问题。

3. 基于专利权利要求的我国新能源汽车产业的保护特色问题

从世界范围来看，新能源汽车作为未来汽车产业的发展方向和制高点，各国都高度重视。发达国家依靠强大的工业能力和储备的高端技术人员在新能源汽车技术方面处于领先地位。例如，日本主要走的是混合动力汽车技术路线，在该领域名列世界前茅，并且研发出能够

---

❶ 《中华人民共和国专利法》第2条。

大规模应用的油电混合动力技术，日本的汽车企业，如
丰田也牢牢掌握了世界尖端的混合动力汽车技术，专利
授权量惊人，并且在中国的专利申请和授权量占据绝大
比例。美国研发的重点是氢燃料电池汽车和可充电式混
合动力汽车，并开始大规模推广乙醇燃料汽车。欧洲在
混合动力技术、纯电动汽车技术和氢燃料汽车方面进行
全方位研发，同时在生物柴油汽车产业化应用领域居世
界领先地位。可见，我国新能源汽车产业在发达国家的
夹缝中艰难的生存着，整个产业技术特色不够突出，核
心技术较少，技术壁垒使得我国新能源产业的技术创新
之路变得异常艰难，从而制约我国新能源汽车产业的发
展。权利要求书反映专利权的保护范围。独立权利要求
应当从整体上反映发明或者实用新型的技术方案，记载
解决技术问题的必要技术特征；从属权利要求应当用附
加的技术特征，对引用的权利要求作进一步限定。专利
申请中，权利要求的撰写关系到专利技术的保护范围的
大小，是非常关键的环节，新能源汽车产业专利技术也
不例外。因此，我国新能源汽车产业不仅要从专利主题
方面重视技术研发方向，而且要强调专利申请权利要求
的撰写，尽量扩大我国新能源汽车产业专利技术的保护
范围，在重点核心技术有所突破。

4. 基于创新主体的我国新能源汽车产业的领军企业问题

目前，我国新能源汽车产业缺少强有力的领军企业。我国新能源汽车产业的专利技术发展仍然以中小企业为主，而且各企业各自发展研发自己的专利技术，力量分散，容易造成重复与浪费。随着外国技术强国纷纷加大新能源汽车技术在华布局力度，国内企业各技术领域专利分布零散，缺少有效的资源整合，竞争力愈发薄弱。此外，由于我国为汽车工业配套的相关产业落后，导致为新能源汽车开发提供原材料与零部件的产业滞后，尚未形成有一定生产能力的产业链。而且，市场需求是新能源汽车发展的基础，市场需求的主体是消费者。目前，国家对新能源汽车产业有一定的政策支持，但这些政策大体上都是针对生产企业的，对新能源汽车消费群体，国家尚未制定完善的鼓励政策。由于目前的新能源汽车售价普遍比传统汽车高出1~2倍，在这种情况下，如果国家补贴不足，市场需求必然会受到很大影响，从而间接影响企业利润，降低企业对新能源汽车的开发热情。当然，最重要的是，政府应该优化扶持政策，扶持有潜力的新能源汽车产业中的重要企业，尽快成为该产业重点领军企业，带动整个产业发展。

近年来，我国逐渐认识到新能源汽车产业未来发展的必要性与必然性，推出一系列措施推动新能源汽车产业化，但是这绝不能仅仅依靠政府补贴扶持、科研机构埋头苦干、媒体宣传炒作即可成事，必须依靠开展自主研发的汽车企业脚踏实地，以世界新能源汽车产业技术发展现状为基础，进行有针对性的研发，力求掌握实质性核心技术，配合合理的专利战略布局，避免因知识产权风险带来对未来汽车产业发展的致命性错误。

（五）小　结

传统汽车产业的落后，让中国在新能源汽车产业超越西方发达国家显得尤为重要。尽管中国在新能源汽车产业的技术方面存在某些差距，但是在新能源汽车产业方面，中国与世界先进水平的差距相对于传统汽车产业的差距要小许多。从目前中国与美国市场上所销售的新能源汽车数量来看，美国市场的销售数量也比中国汽车市场要多许多。中国与美国等发达国家的差距，其实不是在缩小，而是在逐渐扩大。中国科技部部长万钢在2013年上海国际电动汽车示范城市与产业发展论坛发言称，中国政府对电动车产业的支持毫不动摇。政府介入是必需的，而且政府必须强力介入。❶ 政府如何介入，

---

❶ 张志勇："中国新能源汽车需要政府强力介入"，载中国新能源汽车产业网 http://www.xnyqc.ibicn.com/news/d869878.html, 2014-06-21。

介入的依据是什么，这些问题值得思考。本研究报告通过对新能源汽车产业奇瑞、比亚迪、吉利和长安四家企业重点技术领域授权专利布局的分析结果对政府介入提供一定的参考。本部分分析得出如下结论：混合动力领域，奇瑞、比亚迪、吉利专利授权量相差不大，整体专利质量较高，长安授权专利技术水平较低；纯电动汽车领域，各企业发展较为均衡，整体优势较为突出，专利授权量差距极端化不明显，比亚迪处于领先地位，但奇瑞以质量取胜；燃料电池汽车领域，专利授权量总体偏低，专利分布不均，极端化现象明显；在电池技术领域，整体授权量较高，是专利布局的重点领域，但各企业专利布局差距明显。同时，也发现了我国新能源汽车产业的主要企业在专利布局、专利结构、专利特色和专利技术领军企业等方面存在的问题。

六、我国战略性新兴产业专利竞争态势和合作模式及问题[*]
——以新一代信息技术产业中华为、联想、中兴和大唐专利许可为例

新一代信息技术产业是我国战略性新兴产业重点发展的七大产业之一，具有创新活跃、渗透性强、带动作用大等特点，被普遍认为是引领未来经济、科技和社会发展的一支重要力量。把握信息技术升级换代和产业融合发展机遇，加快建设宽带、融合、安全、泛在的下一代信息网络，突破超高速光纤与无线通信、物联网、云计算、数字虚拟、先进半导体和新型显示等新一代信息技术，推进信息技术创新、新兴应用拓展和网络建设的互动结合，创新产业组织模式，提高新型装备保障水平，培育新兴服务业态，增强国际竞争能力，带动我国信息产业实现由大到强的转变。我国新一代信息技术产业发展已迎来难得的历史机遇。（1）发展环境日趋完

---

* 本部分内容由乔永忠和刘思汶共同创作完成，主要内容发表于《中外知识产权评论》2015年第1期，标题为"新一代信息技术产业专利许可实证研究——以华为、联想、中兴和大唐为例"。

善。国务院相关部门已经积极制定相关专项发展规划和政策措施，推进相关领域的改革和制度建设，为新一代信息技术产业发展营造良好环境。（2）信息网络建设和技术演进不断加快。宽带、泛在、融合、安全的新一代信息网络发展正加速推进，物联网、云计算等新兴业态的技术创新和产业化方兴未艾，新兴服务模式不断涌现。（3）国内市场需求潜力巨大。随着我国工业化、信息化、城镇化、市场化、国际化的深入发展，经济结构转型升级和经济社会各领域信息化建设的加快，为新一代信息技术提供了广阔的市场空间。❶ 2013年，新一代信息技术产业平稳发展，软件与电子信息制造两大主要产业平均增速为13.5%，在创新带动下，产业结构调整明显。（1）在国务院出台信息消费政策的鼓励下，软件服务业创新不断，规模快速增长。国内首支互联网基金天弘增利宝（余额宝）上线仅半年规模已突破1 800亿元，开户数超4 000万。大数据、云计算、移动互联网等快速发展，2013年，信息技术咨询服务、数据处理和运行服务收入均取得30%以上增长，带动软件业务收入同比增长24.6%。（2）制造业结构调整，部分行业创新不足，面临困境，如微型计算机和彩色电视机产量同比均出现

---

❶ 国家发展和改革委员会："发展新一代信息技术产业助推结构优化"，载 http://www.ce.cn/xwzx/gnsz/gdxw/201204/26/t20120426_23276350.shtml, 2014-06-21。

负增长。而技术领先行业脱颖而出，我国主导的TD-LTE（增强型时分同步长期演进）技术开始规模商用，4G产业快速发展，带动通信设备制造业主营收入同比增长20.2%，较2012年提升6.1个百分点。❶

随着全球范围内战略性新兴产业的迅速发展，企业围绕专利的竞争与合作形式更加复杂。一方面，由于战略性新兴产业的发展依赖于共性关键技术的突破，以专利为纽带的创新合作更加多样，新型技术创新联盟和专利联盟不断涌现。另一方面，新技术突破和市场策略变化致使专利纠纷愈加频繁。在新形势下，专利竞争态势的复杂性将前所未有，同时专利技术合作的创新模式的多样性也将日新月异。但是作为课题研究报告，因为时间和人力有限，不能将这些复杂性和多样性全部囊括其中，考虑到课题研究的针对性和精准性，本研究报告只选择战略性新兴产业中的新一代信息技术产业为产业研究对象，以其中的四家代表性企业的相关专利数据为研究依据，从专利诉讼视角研究专利竞争态势，以专利许可视角研究专利合作模式，进而观察战略性新兴产业专利市场竞争格局。由此深入分析我国战略性新兴产业代表企业的专利竞争态势和合作模式及其存在问题。

---

❶ 国家信息中心信息资源开发部："战略性新兴产业2013年发展形势及2014年展望"，载http://www.sic.gov.cn/News/82/2591.htm，2014-05-31。

（一）新一代信息技术产业及专利许可研究现状

新一代信息技术产业是我国战略性新兴产业重点发展的七大产业之一，电子信息产品制造、信息网络、信息服务和软产业的融合发展，极大地推动了云计算、物联网、移动互联网、新一代移动通信等新兴业态的发展。❶ 新一代信息技术产业处于科技发展的前沿，凭借一家企业单独的力量，往往存在核心技术难以突破，核心知识产权匮乏，研发资金不足等问题，因此，以专利为纽带的创新技术联盟频频出现。我国专利实施许可合同2012年16 052件，2011年21 665件，2010年21 665件，2009年16 383件。❷ 2012 年，新一代信息技术产业国内发明专利授权数量前十位的省市包括广东、北京、台湾、上海、江苏、浙江、四川、陕西、湖北和福建，其中，福建取代山东进入了前十位。排序前十位的省市新一代信息技术产业发明专利授权共11 365 件，占新一代信息技术产业授权的国内发明专利总量的89.87%。2011 ~ 2012 年，新一代信息技术产业国内发明专利授权量省市前十位分布情况变化不大，两年间前十位的省市只有一个发生变化，即2011 年的山东在2012 年被福建

---

❶ 国务院："'十二五'国家战略性新型产业发展规划"，2010年。

❷ 该数据通过对国家知识产权局网站http://www.sipo.gov.cn/tjxx/公布的专利实施许可合同备案登记信息进行检索整理得到。

所取代，进入前十位。对比2011年和2012年各省市占新一代信息技术产业国内发明专利授权数量的比例，可以看出，新一代信息技术产业国内省市授权分布较为集中，主要集中在广东、北京和中国台湾地区。❶

　　新一代信息技术产业处于科技发展前沿，往往存在核心技术难以突破、核心专利匮乏和研发资金不足等问题，因此，以专利为纽带的创新技术联盟频频出现。有关专利合作的研究成果大多是基于经济全球化大环境下国家间的专利合作、❷ 网络化合作模式❸ 和网络技术创新的速度和传播；❹ 有关专利许可的研究成果主要集中在对专利许可价值的评价指标研究、❺ 专利竞赛中合作模式的发展❻ 和企业专利许可风险的规避问题；❼ 另有学者

---

　　❶　国家知识产权局规划发展司："战略性新兴产业授权发明专利统计报告"，载《专利统计简报》2013年第11期，第34～35页。

　　❷　靳茂勤："我国战略性新兴产业国际合作模式初探"，载《亚太经济》2011年第6期，第46～50页。

　　❸　李葳、王宏起："战略性新兴产业的战略联盟网络化合作模式"，载《学习与探究》2011年第3期，第179～181页。

　　❹　R.W. Rycroft, "Does cooperation absorb complexity? Innovation networks and the speed and spread of complex technological innovation, Technol", *in Forecasting Soc. Change* 7 (2007): 565～578.

　　❺　梁军："中国发明专利许可价值衡量指标研究"，载《电子知识产权》2011年第5期，第52～55页。

　　❻　Silipo, Damiano B. "The Evolution of Cooperation in Patent Races: Theory and Experimental Evidence", *Journal of Economics* 85(2005), *Issue* 1, pp.1～38. 38p. 1Diagram, 4 Charts, 4 Graphs.

　　❼　张曼："企业专利许可风险的规避探析"，载《商业经济评论》2012年第5期，第54～55页。

研究了通信产业技术标准中专利许可收益问题[1]和垄断协议与专利许可交叉问题，[2]通过代表企业对专利合作竞争关系进行分析；[3]基于某一产业领域，通过典型企业间专利许可状况分析专利合作的研究成果很少发现。

因此，本研究报告基于我国新一代信息技术产业迅速发展和企业间专利竞争态势愈加激烈和合作模式逐渐复杂等问题，从专利侵权和专利许可角度分析我国新一代信息技术产业企业专利竞争和专利合作模式，为提高企业知识产权运用能力，促进产业发展提供参考。

（二）数据收集与研究对象

1. 数据收集

本部分专利许可数据来自国家知识产权局专利信息服务平台(http://search.cnipr.com/)法律状态栏目。具体方法为，在法律状态公告日一栏中输入搜索"年份"，法律状态一栏中输入"许可"，然后对搜索结果进行统

---

[1] 徐明："通信产业技术标准中专利许可的收益研究"，载《科学与科学技术管理》2012年第5期，第19~23页。

[2] 穆颖："垄断协议与专利许可交叉问题研究"，载《科技与法律》2013年第4期，第9~13页。

[3] Yu-Shan Chen, Bi-Yu Chen, "Utilizing patent analysis to explore the cooperative competition relationship of the two LED companies: Nichia and Osram", *in Technological Forecasting & Social Change*, 78(2005): 294~302.

计、归类与整合得到。将通过上述方法收集到的申请号输入网站首页的"申请（专利）号"栏目，得到分类号，然后根据IPC（第八版）进行整理即可得到技术领域部分数据。收集数据的时间为2009~2013年。❶

2. 研究对象

根据国家工业和信息化部公布的"2012电子信息百强名单"并参考各企业的主要业务方向，本研究报告从新一代信息技术产业中选取华为技术有限公司（以下简称"华为"）、联想移动通信技术有限公司（以下简称"联想"）、中兴通讯股份有限公司（以下简称"中兴"）和大唐电信科技集团（以下简称"大唐"）四家企业为代表，对其从专利许可量逐年变化、许可对象、许可方式及许可使用专利技术领域等方面对比分析，研究新一代信息技术产业的企业间专利合作模式。

基于我国新一代信息技术产业的迅速发展和企业间合作模式的逐渐复杂化等问题，本部分从专利许可的角度对我国新一代信息技术产业企业间的合作模式及存在的问题进行分析，研究新一代信息技术产业企业专利合作模式。

---

❶ 湖南省知识产权局：《战略性新兴产业专利检索手册》，知识产权出版社2013年版，第426~494页。

（三）新一代信息产业四大企业专利许可数量发展趋势

将专利许可数量按照年份统计，得到华为、联想、中兴和大唐公司的专利许可数量变化趋势（见表6-1）。

表6-1 2008～2013年四家代表企业专利许可量分布　　（件）

年份	2009年	2010年	2011年	2012年	2013年
华为	23	6	10	1	0
中兴	47	3	13	5	1
联想	0	0	5	15	68
大唐	9	4	7	1	2

从表6-1看出以下两种趋势：（1）除联想外，四家企业专利许可数量呈现波浪式递减趋势。（2）联想专利许可量呈现逐年递增趋势。2009年和2010年没有专利许可记录，2011年开始逐渐出现少量专利许可，2013年剧增，截至4月达到68件；华为、中兴和大唐的许可量都呈现逐年递减的趋势，2009年专利许可量最多，2013年华为无专利许可记录。

联想专利许可量在2013年激增和其与杜比的合作历程相关，联想的专利许可几乎全部来自杜比实验室。自2005年起，杜比与联想开始携手合作，不断推出具有强大娱乐功能和影院级音响体验体验的PC产品。2008年，在联想全新系列的IdeaPad笔记本电脑中，全系列采用了

"杜比家庭影院技术"，集合了联想全球创新技术和设计实力的IdeaPad笔记本电脑，将"杜比家庭影院技术"的优质体验，为全球消费笔记本用户所享。然而真正意义上的专利许可从2012年6月杜比实验室与联想公司达成一项为期两年的合作协议开始，之后联想在ThinkPad、Think Centre、IdeaPad和Idea Centre等产品线中采用第四代杜比家庭影院技术或第二代杜比PC先进音频技术，从而使得2013年联想的专利许可量激增。

（四）新一代信息产业四大企业许可专利类型

四家企业中除中兴许可专利有5件外观设计专利外，其余企业许可专利都是发明专利或实用新型专利，其专利类型分为产品、方法和产品及方法（见表6-2）。许可专利类型中华为和大唐主要为产品及方法专利，联想产品专利居多，中兴三种类型分布均匀。究其原因，与各企业的业务分布关系密切，华为产品和解决方案涵盖移动、宽带、IP、光网络、电信增值业务和终端等领域，致力于提供全IP融合解决方案，因此涉及的方法专利多于产品专利；联想是全球个人电脑市场的领导企业，主要生产台式电脑、服务器、笔记本电脑、打印机、掌上电脑、主板、手机等商品，许可专利的类型多集中于产品专利；中兴是全球领先的综合通信解决方案提供商，全球第四大手机生产制造商，两块业务比重相当，反映出其许可专利中产品专利和方法专利的比重基本持平；大唐的主要业务包括通信终端产业和与通信终端相协调的通信应用和服务产业两大部分，因而许可专利的内容也同时涉及产品和方法两个方面。可见，企业许可专利类型与其主要经营业务相关。

表6-2　四家企业许可专利类型　　　　（件）

	华为	联想	中兴	大唐
产品及方法	22	27	23	11
方法	11	18	23	8
产品	7	43	23	4

（五）新一代信息产业四大企业许可专利的技术领域

通过对许可专利根据IPC分类号进行技术领域划分，可以掌握四家企业技术的输出和需求程度。本部分根据IPC（第八版），分析四家企业许可专利涉及的技术领域分布。❶ 信息技术产业的IPC分类号主要分布在G部和H部，也有少量分布在B部和C部。❷

---

❶　一件专利的申请号可能对应一个或多个IPC分类号。

❷　湖南省知识产权局：《战略性新兴产业专利检索手册》，知识产权出版社2013年版，第426～494页。

1. 许可专利按部划分

对许可专利按照部进行分类，可以粗略了解四大企业专利许可的领域。四家企业许可专利整体分布如下：华为许可专利技术分布在H（电学）部的有50件，G（物理）部26件、B（作业；运输）部1件、C（化学；冶金）部1件；联想许可专利技术分布在H部55件、G部52件；中兴许可专利技术分布在H部111件、G部22件；大唐许可专利技术分布在H部39件、G部6件、C部6件。

从四家企业整体的技术分布情况来看，专利许可技术主要集中在H部，其次是G部，C部和B部技术也有少量涉及。

2. 许可专利按大类划分

对四家企业许可专利按照大类划分整理，得到其许可专利技术的分布情况（见表6-3）。华为的专利许可分布较为分散，其他三家企业则相对集中，主要集中在H04大类（电通信技术）。

首先，华为许可专利技术分布相对均匀，主要集中在G10大类（乐器、声学），其次在H05大类（其他类目不包含的电技术）和H04大类（电通信技术）分布较多。其次，与华为不同，其他三家企业许可专利的技术领域分布相对集中：联想主要分布在H04大类（电通信技术）和H03大类（基本电子电路）；中兴主要集中在H04大类

（电通信技术），少量分布在G06大类（计算机、推算、计数）；大唐也主要集中在H04大类（电通信技术），在G01大类（测量、测试）领域有少量专利许可。

表6-3 四大企业许可专利按照大类技术领域分布 （件）

	华为	联想	中兴	大唐
基本电器元件（H01）	8	—	3	—
发电、变电或配电（H02）	7	—	4	—
基本电子电路（H03）	1	20	3	1
电通信技术（H04）	15	35	102	40
其他类目不包含的电技术（H05）	17			
测量；测试（G01）	11	—	2	3
控制；调节（G05）	1		2	
计算机；推算；计数（G06）	13	9	14	2
信号装置（G08）	2			
乐器；声学（G10）	40	—	3	1
信息存储（G11）	3			
测时学（G04）	—	—	1	—

　　华为是信息与通信解决方案供应商，在电信网络、企业网络、消费者和云计算等领域构筑端到端的解决方案，为电信运营商、企业和消费者等提供ICT解决方案和服务，业务范围广泛，因此其许可专利的技术分布情况比较分散，并且在G10大类（乐器、声学）、H05大类（其他类目不包含的电技术）和H04大类（电通信技术）的技术相对突出。

联想集团由联想及前IBM个人电脑事业部所组成，开发、制造和销售科技产品及服务，产品线包括个人电脑服务器、工作站以及包括平板电脑和智能手机等的一系列移动互联网终端，因此技术内容主要集中在对互联网终端的开发上，涉及最多的技术领域是H04大类（电通信技术）和H03大类（基本电子电路）。

中兴技术领域集中的表现可能与其仍处在转型初期密切相关，在中兴全球分析师大会上，中兴执行副总裁何士友曾表示："从2012年及之后三年，中兴将着重从电信设备提供商向通信综合服务提供商转型，致力于不断将产品与服务进行融合，从而满足多种类型市场的需求。"这使得中兴现阶段的技术仍高度集中在H04大类（电通信技术）。

大唐的情况与中兴类似，大唐电信正在深化调整公司的产业结构和产品结构，战略布局并大力发展战略新兴产业，将发展重点由核心网向更靠近用户的领域转移，由提供单一产品向整体解决方案转型。

3. 许可专利按小类划分

四家企业许可专利小类涉及技术领域的主要分布如表6-4所示。

表6-4 四家企业许可专利主要涉及的技术领域及其数量 （件）

华为	H01B	H01L	H02H	H04B	H04L	H05K	G01R	G06F	G06Q	G08G
	3	4	6	4	11	17	11	12	2	2
联想	H03G	H03M	H04B	H04N	H04R	H04S	G06F	G10K	G10L	G11B
	13	7	5	6	6	16	7	4	36	3
中兴	H02H	H02J	H03M	H04B	H04J	H04L	H04M	H04N	H04Q	G06F
	2	2	2	11		16	10		35	14
大唐	H04B	H04L	H04M	H04Q	H04W	G01S	G06F	G10L	B65D	—
	4	12	6	14	2	3	2	2	3	

B26D：切割或用于切断；H01B：电缆、导体或绝缘体及其选择；H01L：半导体器件等；H02H：紧急保护电路装置；H02J：供电或配电电路装置或系统；H03G：放大的控制；H03M：一般编码、译码或代码转换；H04B：传输；H04J：多路复用通信；H04L：数字信息的传输；H04M：电话通信；H04N：图像通信；H04Q：选择；H04R：扬声器、助听器及扩音系统等；H04S：立体声系统；G10K：发声器械；G10L：语音合成或识别；H05K：印刷电路；G01R：测量电或磁变量；G01S：无线电导航等；G06F：电数字数据处理；G06Q：数据处理系统或方法等；G08G：交通控制系统；G10L：音频分析或处理等；G11B：基于记录载体和换能器之间的相对运动而实现的信息存储。

　　从表6-4可得出如下结论：华为许可专利涉及技术领域最多的是H05K小类（印刷电路等），其次是G06F（电数字数据处理）H04L小类（数字信息的传输）和G01R（测量电或磁变量）；联想许可专利涉及技术领域中G10L小类语音合成或识别相对于其他小类遥遥领先，其余小类如H04S（立体声系统）和H03G（放大的控制）等则分布均匀，均有一定量的分布；中兴❶许可专利涉

---

　　❶ 中兴许可专利中有5件外观设计的分类号未在表格中列出。

及的技术领域中小类H04Q（选择）的总量最高，除此之外H04L(数字信息的传输)、G06F（电数字数据处理）、H04B（传输）等均有一定量的分布；大唐的许可专利涉及的技术领域主要有H04Q（选择）、H04L（数字信息的传输）和H04M（电话通信）。

（六）新一代信息产业四大企业专利（被）许可地位

通过分析四家企业专利（被）许可人（见表6-5[1]），分析各企业许可模式异同。华为的专利许可的被许可人不固定，大多是广东省的公司。华为是全球第二大通信设备供应商、全球第三大智能手机厂商，也是全球领先的信息与通信解决方案供应商。随着华为企业逐渐走向成熟，在国内的专利许可量逐年减少，然而同时华为每年支付3亿美元左右的专利许可费，以获得业界其他公司专利技术的合法使用权。目前，华为已经与业界主要厂商和专利权持有人签署了数十份知识产权交叉许可协议。华为的专利合作模式正向我们展现了一个在国内基本成熟的大企业与国外技术领先企业专利许可合作的过程。

---

[1] 四家企业的信息来自各企业官方网站。

表6-5　四家企业在许可中的地位			（件）
	华为	联想	中兴	大唐
许可	40	3	67	30
被许可	0	85	2	0

在联想的88件许可专利中，有3件是联想移动通信科技有限公司对联想移动通信软件（武汉）有限公司关于终端设备的专利许可使用；其余85件都是被许可使用，并且许可人是固定的杜比实验室特许公司、杜比国际公司，其中有33件是杜比实验室特许公司、杜比国际公司对联想移动通信科技有限公司的专利许可使用，52件是杜比实验室特许公司、杜比国际公司对联想（北京）有限公司的专利许可使用。杜比实验室特许公司、杜比国际公司主要发明声音降噪及声音压缩编码等技术，这正与联想的产品需要相契合，杜比数字技术是世界上最为先进的音频编码系统，美国、欧盟、澳大利亚等国家和地区几乎都把杜比数字作为其数字电视传输标准中音频部分的首选，杜比实验室特许公司、杜比国际公司不仅提供技术认证服务，而且为企业提供音频技术的全套解决方案，帮助企业开发新产品，开拓新市场。联想与杜比实验室特许公司、杜比国际公司通过专利许可使用达成专利合作，保证技术更新与企业发展同步进行，这无

疑是联想能够迅速发展壮大的坚实的技术后盾。

中兴专利许可，大部分为许可他人使用专利，其中许可内部公司使用的专利许可量占总量的81%，其余与其他企业间的许可只占19%。中兴专利许可的许可人均为中兴通讯股份有限公司；除此之外，有2件专利许可是意大利息思维有限责任公司对中兴通讯股份有限公司的专利许可使用。近年来中兴对专利技术的把握上升到一个新的高度，2013年第一季度，中兴通讯的国际专利申请量继续位居全球企业第一，这些专利的申请地则覆盖了欧美、日本、韩国和一些经济发展迅猛的新兴国家。在过去五年中，中兴在欧美市场的营业收入增长近50%，出口的快速增长得益于专利技术的有力支撑，取决于总公司与子公司和分公司间快速的技术交流，因此对于中兴来说，企业内部的专利许可比与其他企业间的专利许可更为重要。

大唐的专利许可对象情况与中兴类似，多为企业内部的专利许可使用，这与大唐复杂的内部组织结构是分不开的。大唐的专利许可的许可人全部为大唐集团的下属企业，主要有西安大唐电信有限公司、大唐移动通信设备有限公司、大唐微电子技术有限公司、大唐电信科技股份有限公司、电信科学技术研究院和大唐微电子技术有限公司；被许可方也基本都是大唐集团的内部企业，包括大唐电信（天津）技术服务有限公司、大唐电信(天津)通信终端制造有限公司、大唐电信科技产业控股有限公司和电信科学技术第四研究所,除此之外大唐集团对外其他公司的专利使用许可有2件,分别是上海飞利通信科技实业总公司和广州市明森机电设备有限公司。

(七)新一代信息产业四大企业专利许可方式

专利实施许可按许可方所授予被许可方的权利和范围大小,可分为独占许可、排他许可、普通许可、分许可、交叉许可。

华为的许可类型全部为独占许可,没有普通许可;联想的许可方式以普通许可为主,有85件,占总许可量的96.59%,独占许可仅3件;中兴的许可方式主要是独占许可,共66件,占总量的97.06%,普通许可只有2件;大唐的许可方式中独占许可也占了大部分,共19件,占总量的90.48%,普通许可2件。四家企业专利许可类型主要的许可方式只有独占许可和普通许可两种类型,华为、中兴和大唐的独占许可方式占绝对多数,联想的情况则相反(见表6-6)。

独占许可只有被许可人可以使用许可人的专利,其他人包括许可人本人均不得使用该专利,这种许可方式能为企业节约管理成本,目的性强,适用于企业之间的合作。华为、中兴和大唐的专利许可基本都是企业之间的许可，因此独占许可居多。与此相反，联想的专利许可中绝大多数都来自杜比实验室特许公司、杜比国际公司，相当于杜比实验室特许公司、杜比国际公司为联想提供技术支持，所以更多适用普通许可。专利许可的类型因合作的对象和合作方式的不同而不同，华为、中兴和大唐以独占许可为主，而联想则普通许可居多。

表6-6　四家企业专利许可类型分布　　　（件）

	华为	联想	中兴	大唐
独占许可	40	3	68	20
普通许可	0	85	2	2

综上所述，得出以下五点结论：（1）四家企业专利许可数量总体上呈现逐年递减的趋势，联想例外；（2）许可专利类型中华为和大唐主要为产品及方法专利，联想产品专利居多，中兴三种类型分布均匀；（3）许可专利涉及技术领域最多的分别是华为在H05K小类（印刷电路等）、联想在G10L小类（音频分析或处理等）、中兴和大唐在小类H04Q（选择）；（4）在（被）许可人方面中兴的专利许可大部分为企业内部的许可；联想和大唐的专利许可人比较固定；华为的被许可人不固定，大多是广东省的公司；（5）四家企业专利许可类型只有独占许可和普通许可两种类型，华为、中兴和大唐的独占许

可方式占绝对多数，联想情况则相反。

从上文的分析可以得出在电子信息产业中，随着企业的成熟化，专利的布局越来越严谨，需要被许可和许可其他企业实施专利数量呈现逐年减少的现象，更多的是企业内部不同公司间的专利实施许可，这种情况下的许可方式多为独占许可。而发展处于上升阶段的企业的专利被许可实施量则增势明显，在某个技术领域发展较快而专利的研发跟不上的情况下，也可能会选择与某些固定的公司进行专利合作，这种情况下许可的方式多为普通许可。不同企业的产品、方法、产品及方法专利许可类型存在明显差异，许可专利涉及技术领域大类相似，小类差异显著。企业在专利许可中所处地位不同，专利许可主要类型相同，但具体许可专利数量存在显著不同。

（八）新一代信息技术产业专利许可现状及原因

在中国的新一代信息技术产业中，随着企业的成熟化，专利的布局越来越严谨，通过对华为、联想、中兴和大唐的专利许可数据进行整理我们可以梳理出新一代信息技术产业专利合作中存在的问题。

（1）国内大型企业与其他企业之间通过专利许可模式进行合作的现象逐渐减少，正在进一步开展与国外技术领先企业的专利合。专利许可可以弥补企业技术支持上的不足，使企业保证一定的发展速度，同时可以保证先进的技术被充分利用，促进科技的发展进步。我国专利许可立法方面的不足使得企业在进行专利许可的过程中没有固定的规范可以遵循，比较容易产生纠纷，给专利许可制度的运转带来很大阻力，无法发挥其应有的优势，进而无法形成全面的专利联盟格局，使得近几年的专利许可量呈现出不增反减的趋势。因此，进一步完善专利许可方面的立法，形成严密的法律体系是解决这一问题的根本途径。

（2）随着企业规模不断扩大，集团内部与下属企业或子公司之间的专利许可不断增多，而发展处于上升阶段的企业的专利被许可实施量则增势明显，在某个技术领域发展较快而专利的研发滞后的情况下，也可能会选择与某些固定的研发公司进行专利合作。

（3）我国新一代信息技术产业的技术相对世界一流水平而言仍然滞后，企业仍处于扩大规模的初级阶段，内部各个公司间还没有达到技术同步。近年来，我国信息技术产业发展日新月异，飞快的发展速度同时也带来了企业内部技术水平分布不均等问题，在技术发展的同时企业本身也在不断壮大，但核心的技术内容往往只由母公司掌握，分公司或子公司在使用的时候要通过母公司的专利许可，这无疑给企业内部技术融合、进行整体的专利布局带来了不便，同时也成为集团内部与下属企业或子公司之间的专利许可不断增多的原因。

（4）信息技术产业专利许可方式单一，绝大多数为普通许可和独占许可。专利实施许可按许可方所授予被许可方的权利和范围大小，可分为独占许可、排他许可、普通许可、分许可、交叉许可。从前文的分析结果可以看出，信息技术产业在专利许可方式上仍然比较保守，集中在普通许可和独占许可两种相对基本的专利许可方式，四家代表企业在排他许可、分许可和交叉许可三种方式上尚无记录。其根本原因在于专利许可方式方面的立法尚不成熟，普通许可和独占许可相对于其他三种许可方式更加便于操作，然而分许可和交叉许可是基本许可方式的叠加，正确运用可以很大程度上节约操作成本。因此，企业要提高效率，就要尝试运用复杂的专利许可方式，根据不同的情形合理地运用不同的许可方式。

（九）小　结

新一代信息技术产业发展的主要内容是"加快建设宽带、泛在、融合、安全的信息网络基础设施，推动新一代移动通信、下一代互联网核心设备和智能终端的研发及产业化，加快推进三网融合，促进物联网、云计算的研发和示范应用。着力发展集成电路、新型显示、高端软件、高端服务器等核心基础产业。提升软件服务、网络增值服务等信息服务能力，加快重要基础设施智能化改造。大力发展数字虚拟等技术，促进文化创意产业发展"。❶ 其中与通信业有关的是宽带网络、新一代移动通信（TD-LTE及其后续标准4G）、下一代互联网核心设备和智能终端、三网融合、物联网等。在新的国际背景下，该产业专利竞争态势和合作模式在一定程度上决定了其发展的水平。本部分通过对我国新一代信息技术产业四个重要企业专利许可方面的合作模式分析，得出以下五点结论：（1）四家企业专利许可数量总体上呈现逐年递减的趋势，联想例外；（2）许可专利类型中华为和中兴主要为产品及方法专利，联想产品专利居多，中兴三种类型分布均匀；（3）许可专利涉及技术领域最多的分别是华为在H05K小类（印刷电路等）、联想在G10L小类（音频分析或处理等）、中兴和大唐在小类H04Q（选择）；（4）在（被）许可人方面中兴的专利许可大部分为企业内部的许可；联想和大唐的专利许可人比较固定；华为的被许可人不固定，大多是广东省的公司；（5）四家企业专利许可类型只有独占许可和普通许可

---

❶ 国务院办公厅："国务院关于加快培育和发展战略性新兴产业的决定"，国发〔2010〕32号，载中央政府门户网站http://www.gov.cn/zwgk/2010-10/18/content_1724848.htm, 2014-06-21。

两种类型，华为、中兴和大唐的独占许可方式占绝对多数，联想情况则相反。

七、运用专利制度促进我国战略性新兴产业发展的对策

    国家知识产权局原局长田力普曾提出从以下几方面加强战略性新兴产业的知识产权工作。（1）积极创造知识产权，知识产权数量、质量和结构并举。通过建立重大经济科技活动知识产权审议制度、构建科学有效的评价指标体系、完善知识产权申请与审查制度等措施，引导企业和研发机构形成科学有效的知识产权布局。（2）有效运用知识产权。积极拓展知识产权投融资方式、创新知识产权金融产品。创新知识产权转移转化形式，大力开展知识产权运营综合体系建设，完善知识产权交易政策和市场交易体系。（3）科学管理知识产权。在产业集聚区积极探索知识产权集群管理模式，构建形成企业有序创新、合作创新的发展格局。将企业知识产权管理能力提升作为重要切入点，鼓励创建知识产权优势企业，加强企业知识产权信息运用水平和知识产权服务体系建设。（4）依法保护知识产权。密切关注战略性新兴产业发展动向，制定有针对性的知识产权保护政策。大力支持企业和研发机构在国外部署知识产权，鼓励其在国外

运用知识产权。加大国外知识产权维权援助力度，健全和完善相关知识产权预警应急机制、国外维权和争端解决机制，指导企业及时有效获得知识产权保护。[1] 本书认为，在上述要求基础上，企业、高等院校、研究机构以及各级政府应该充分发挥和运用知识产权制度，支持战略性新兴产业健康、快速和可持续发展，本书就如何运用专利制度促进我国战略性新兴产业发展，提出如下对策。

（一）完善专利制度及政策，促进战略性新兴产业可持续发展

1. 区分不同产业或技术领域专利政策，促进战略性新兴产业有序发展

战略性新兴产业包含的范围较广，从国家层面上包括环保、信息、生物、高端装备制造、新能源、新材料和新能源汽车等技术领域，不同地区又根据本地区技术优势和经济发展水平界定了该地区战略性新兴产业的范围。不同领域中技术创新的特点不同，因此对于知识产权政策有着不同的需求。2007年，欧洲专利局发布的

---

[1] 田力普："知识产权是培育和发展战略性新兴产业的关键"，载《经济日报》2012年5月4日。

《未来知识产权制度愿景》指出，包括强制许可制度在内的一些灵活机制可能在战略性新兴产业中与环境相关领域发挥作用。❶ 美国联邦巡回上诉法院（CAFC）有时也根据不同行业技术创新的不同特点，对知识产权法进行斟酌适用。❷ 因此，建议根据战略性新兴产业中不同技术领域的特点，制定并适用分领域、有区别的专利政策，进一步促进战略性新兴产业的健康发展。

2. 通过专利加快审查制度切实增强战略性新兴产业专利优势

我国对于战略性新兴产业核心技术的专利申请实施依请求的加快审查制度，即专利申请人可以请求对于涉及战略性新兴产业核心技术的专利申请予以加快实质审查和优先复审审查，有利于我国创新主体尽早在战略性新兴产业核心技术领域形成竞争优势，有利于构建我国在该领域的核心竞争力。建立专利加快审查制度，对我国战略性新兴产业发展有如下两点好处：（1）提高战略性新兴产业专利审查的质量和效率。适当加快战略性新兴产业的关键行业和重要领域的专利审查过程，可以加速技术产业化的进程。（2）根据战略性新兴产业发展需

---

❶ EPO, "Scenarios for the future", in. http://www.epo.org/news-issues/issues/scenarios/download. html, last retrieved on July 4, 2011.

❷ 毛金生、程文婷："战略性新兴产业知识产权政策初探"，载《知识产权》2011年第9期，第63~69页。

要，合理限定专利权利要求范围。例如，在基因技术领域，如果对于基因序列保护范围过大，将会带来垄断问题；对于研究工具的保护，也会对社会公众利益带来不利影响。❶ 因此，对战略性新兴产业中的技术进行专利审查时，要充分考虑我国国情，予以适当限定。

3. 通过完善专利费用资助制度解决战略性新兴产业知识产权管理资金困难

我国目前专利费用资助制度包括两类：国家知识产权局实施的针对缴费确有困难的专利申请人或者专利权人的普遍减缓制度；地方政府实施的针对本地专利申请人或者专利权人的专利费用无偿资助制度。国家知识产权局实施的普遍减缓制度伴随着专利制度得以建立，地方政府实施的无偿资助制度从1999年开始试行，目前已经为绝大多数地方政府普遍实施。国家知识产权局在2008年1月21日下发《关于专利申请资助工作的指导意见》，推动地方政府实施的专利费用无偿资助制度加以完善。财政部于2009年8月28日下发《资助向国外申请专利专项资金管理暂行办法》，对向国外提出的专利申请加以资助，以引导我国企业构建核心竞争力，积极拓展海外市场。可以说，借助对我国创新主体的公共财政资

---

❶ 张鹏："战略性新兴产业发展的知识产权制度回应"，载《中国发明与专利》2011年第9期，第19～24页。

助，引导和激励了我国创新主体的创新方向。战略性新兴产业核心技术是我国着力发展的创新方向之一，代表了未来先进技术和经济模式的方向。借鉴向国外提出的专利申请的资助制度，实施战略性新兴产业核心技术专利申请的专项资助，积极引导我国创新主体对于战略性新兴产业核心技术发明创造的积极性，推动我国创新主体占据战略性新兴产业核心技术的核心竞争力。❶战略性新兴产业需要投入大量的研发资金，而投入该产业知识产权管理的相关费用相对较少，这是一个比较普遍的问题，通过完善专利资助费用制度可以在一定程度上解决战略性新兴产业相关企业知识产权管理资金困难问题。

（二）通过提升专利创造水平，强化战略性 新兴产业发展基础

1. 通过获取核心技术的高质量专利提高战略性新兴产业竞争力

为了夯实我国战略性新兴产业的发展基础，获得核心技术的高质量专利至少要重视以下两个方面的问题。

---

❶ 张鹏："战略性新兴产业发展的知识产权制度回应"，载《中国发明与专利》2011年第9期，第19～24页。

（1）强化战略性新兴产业关键核心技术专利的创造和取得。要在未来国际竞争中占据有利地位，必须加快培育和发展战略性新兴产业，切实完善创新机制，提升技术创新能力，推进原始创新，增强集成创新，参与国际合作，加强引进消化吸收再创新，利用全球创新资源，突破关键核心技术，掌握关键核心技术及相关专利，尤其是发明专利。（2）通过政策引导提高战略性新兴产业专利质量。完善专利评价指标体系，逐步加大知识产权质量和市场价值在相关考核和评价中的权重，引导创新主体以市场竞争为导向不断提高专利质量、优化专利结构。

2. 根据战略性新兴产业不同领域发展情况进行专利科学布局

在发展战略性新兴产业过程中，首要任务是发掘具有引领带动作用并且能够实现突破的若干重点技术方向。充分利用现有技术资源，分析战略性新兴产业专利布局，发现技术突破口非常重要。为此，应该对战略性新兴产业专利信息，尤其是专利申请量、授权量，国内外专利申请人分布情况，重点跨国企业专利布局情况，专利的被引用状况，技术标准中的专利纳入情况等进行深入分析，力求发掘最有可能率先突破和做大做强的技术领域，指导企业结合自身技术基础、产业优势以及战略性新兴产业技术发展特点和国内外专利布局状况，加大研发投入和专利布局，有的放矢地开展技术创新和专利申请工作。根据战略性新兴产业专利信息，增强创新主体申请专利的针对性，构筑专利比较优势。推动重大科技项目围绕产业发展制定并实施专利战略，形成符合市场竞争需要的战略性专利组合。

3. 根据企业技术优势，科学制定战略性新兴产业专利技术路线图

专利技术路线图对于提高战略性新兴产业专利管理和运用能力，促进自主创新具有十分重要的作用，所以建议做好以下工作。（1）通过专利技术路线图可以寻找发展战略性新兴产业技术的突破口。近年来，跨国公司不断加大知识产权战略布局，利用"专利先行"实现"跑马圈地"，通过早期的专利布局赢得市场竞争的先机。因此，我国相关创新主体应该组织力量大力开展战略性新兴产业专利信息分析，对战略性新兴产业的专利申请量、授权量，国内外专利申请人分布情况，重点跨国企业专利布局情况，专利的被引用状况，技术标准中的专利纳入情况等进行深入分析，争取发掘出可能率先突破的技术领域，指导企业结合自身技术基础、产业优势以及产业技术发展特点和国内外专利布局状况，加大研发投入和专利布局，避开侵权风险较高的技术领域，

合理开展技术创新和专利申请工作。（2）通过专利技术路线图有助于创新主体在发展战略性新兴产业中了解产业发展基本框架、路线图以及推进方式等。只有以此为依据，才能有针对性地支持重点领域的发展，确定引导企业技术开发的方向，形成自己的技术优势。要抓住当前发展知识产权服务业的契机，在跟踪、检测和预见国际动态的基础上制定战略性新兴产业的专利布局图和技术战略图，从而引导社会各界把创新资源投入到这些关键技术中去。因此，通过专利技术路线图，不仅有助于相关企业从战略高度对战略性新兴产业技术的研发和布局进行前瞻性部署，而且有助于降低战略性新兴产业技术的不确定性和复杂性，提升战略性新兴产业的创新水平和发展速度。

（三）提高专利运用能力，促进战略性新兴产业发展动力和后劲

1. 强化产业和企业专利战略，提升战略性新兴产业发展能力

专利战略管理对战略性新兴产业发展具有非常重要的作用，应该给予足够重视。（1）要加强战略性新兴产业专利战略管理。加快完善期权、技术入股、股权、分红权等多种形式的激励机制，鼓励科研机构和高校科

技人员积极从事职务发明创造。支持知识产权的创造和运用，强化专利保护和管理，鼓励企业建立专利联盟。完善高校和科研机构专利转移转化的利益保障和实现机制，建立高效的专利评估交易机制。加大对具有重大社会效益创新成果的奖励力度。要鼓励我国战略性新兴产业相关企业和研发机构支持或参与国际标准的制定。完善出口信贷、保险等政策，结合对外援助等积极支持战略性新兴产业领域的重点产品、技术和服务开拓国际市场以及自主知识产权技术标准在海外推广应用。（2）加强战略性新兴产业相关企业拥有专利的产业化管理。发挥知识密集型服务业支撑作用，大力发展研发服务、信息服务、创业服务、技术交易、专利和科技成果转化等高技术服务业，推进重大科技成果及其专利产业化和产业集聚发展。完善科技成果产业化机制，加大实施产业化示范工程力度，积极推进重大装备应用。依托具有优势的产业集聚区，培育一批创新能力强、创业环境好、特色突出、集聚发展的战略性新兴产业专利示范园区或企业，形成增长极，辐射带动区域经济发展。

2. 创新专利融资方式和转移转化方式，盘活战略性新兴产业发展资金

拓展专利融资方式和创新专利转移转化方式对战略性新兴产业专利价值的实现十分关键。建议主要做好以

下两方面工作。（1）通过拓展专利投融资方式，实现专利潜在价值。完善专利质押、出资入股、融资担保制度。探索建立专利融资机构，支持中小企业快速成长。加快建立包括财政出资和社会资金投入在内的多层次担保体系。积极发展中小金融机构和新型金融服务。综合运用风险补偿等财政优惠政策，促进金融机构支持战略性新兴产业发展的力度。（2）通过创新专利转移转化形式，促进专利价值实现。促进战略性新兴产业集聚区专利运营综合服务体系建设，培育一批在区域经济发展中发挥重要作用的专利运营机构。探索建立专利拍卖及相关制度。完善专利入股、股权和分红权等形式的激励机制和资产管理制度。完善专利交易政策，建立健全专利评估交易机制，支持设立以专利权转移为重点的技术转移机构，推进专利交易市场体系建设，促进专利交易。加强专利技术组合与商标保护的衔接配套，鼓励运用商标保护专利技术组合产品。

3. 鼓励相关企业建立专利联盟，提升战略性新兴产业整体技术实力

构筑专利联盟是提升企业专利综合实力和反跨国公司技术压制能力的重要手段。为了避免中小企业分散、单兵作战能力的不足，同时防止重复建设，有必要由政府出面，出台专利联盟相关政策，构建战略性新兴产业

专利联盟，以整合创新资源，形成合力，保证整个产业的顺利发展。其重点是实施战略性新兴产业专利联盟试点示范工程。 为此，建议有计划地针对有条件的战略性新兴产业集群，每年扶植若干家专利联盟，通过支持联盟企业构筑专利池、制定实施行业专利战略、建立行业专利预警平台及涉外应对机制、推动专利技术产业化、商品化、标准化，提升产业创新发展水平，形成一批有影响力的战略性新兴产业创新企业群。

4. 完善专利风险预警与评估制度，促进战略性新兴产业健康发展

与传统产业相比，战略性新兴产业的发展具有高风险性，因此对战略性新兴产业核心技术相关项目涉及专利的风险进行预警评估具有重要意义。（1）由政府主导对于重点发展的战略性新兴产业核心技术主要领域的知识产权现状加以分析，并对其中存在的知识产权风险启动预警与评估机制，以便于宏观产业发展政策的制定中充分考虑知识产权因素；（2）战略性新兴产业各产业的重要企业都应该具有专利风险意识，重视各自产业技术发展动向及专利布局，对其可能存在的专利风险提前进行充分的预警分析和评估，大幅度降低战略性新兴产业快速发展过程中的技术风险；（3）要重视战略性新兴产业企业在海外的知识产权预警评估，鼓励企业积极开展

全球研发服务外包，在境外开展联合研发和设立研发机构，在国外申请专利，进行专利布局，为我国企业走向世界做好知识产权准备。

（四）强化专利保护和管理，提升战略性新兴产业发展环境和效率

1. 强化专利保护和执法，优化战略性新兴产业发展环境

任何知识产权运用的前提都是建立在一定程度的知识产权保护基础上，所以要想有高效的知识产权运用，必须具有合理的知识产权保护基础。战略性新兴产业发展环境的优化离不开较为完善的专利保护制度和执法措施。（1）通过完善专利保护法律法规和政策保障战略性新兴产业快速发展。探索制定战略性新兴产业领域新产品、新技术等的专利保护政策，完善相关领域的专利审查标准。积极应对新一代信息技术发展带来的挑战。（2）通过强化专利执法措施优化战略性新兴产业发展环境。强化战略性新兴产业领域专利保护，加大战略性新兴产业专业市场和重大技术标准中的专利保护力度。将战略性新兴产业领域的维权援助纳入全国维权援助机构的中心工作，建立由多元主体共同参与的维权援助体系。

2. 完善产学研用合作创新机制，提高战略性新兴产业发展效率

强化产学研用有效合作是促进战略性新兴产业发展的重要条件之一。针对产学研用合作创新，建议就战略性新兴产业发展主要采取如下措施：（1）完善和强化产学研合作机制，出台相关法规。通过立法突破目前面临的体制机制、合作模式以及人才培养方面的障碍，建立共同投入、成果分享，技术、市场、管理等风险分担机制，推动产学研用合作的可持续发展。（2）建立以市场为导向的产学研用支撑体系。建立和完善产学研用结合统筹协调机制；制定并完善产学研用专项扶持政策；设立产学研用合作专项引导资金；扶持和培育中介服务机构。（3）探索多元化的产学研用合作创新模式。❶构建战略性新兴产业高端产学研用合作创新平台，突破制度性障碍，引导创新要素向战略性新兴产业集聚，是促进战略性新兴产业发展的重要途径之一。

3. 提高专利管理效率，促进战略性新兴产业发展水平

通过专利管理模式的优化形成我国战略性新兴产业竞争优势，主要从以下三方面入手。（1）强化战略性新兴产业集聚区专利产业集群管理。探索建立以战略性新

---

❶ 马德秀："产学研用合作创新推动战略性新兴产业发展"，载《中国科技产业》2011年第1期，第16~17页。

兴产业优势企业为龙头、技术关联企业为主体、专利布局与产业链相匹配的专利集群管理模式。（2）提升战略性新兴产业相关企业专利管理能力。规范企业专利管理标准，建立企业专利管理体系和专利战略实施机制。（3）加强战略性新兴产业专利服务体系建设。分类制定服务标准和服务规范，加强对专利服务机构的服务资质管理和分级分类管理。

参考文献

1 Arora, A., Fosfuri, *A.*Licensing the market technology. *Journal of Economic Behavior & Organization*, 2003 (52):277~295

2 Bingbin Lu. Expedited patent examination for green inventions: Developing countries policy choice. *Energy Policy,* 2013, 61(10): 1529~1538

3 Brent B. A, Walter G. P. The influence of patent protection on firm innovation investment in manufacturing industries. *Journal of International Management*, 2007, 13 (2):91~109

4 Bronwyn H. Hall, Christian Helmers. Innovation and diffusion of clean/green technology: Can patent commons help. *Journal of Environmental Economics and Management*, 2013, (66):33~51

5 Chen Liuqin. Problems and challenges of the new energy vehicle industry in China. *Electricity*, 2012 (2):6~9

6 Cohen, W. M., Goto, A., Nagata, A., Nelson, R. R., & Walsh, J. P. R&D spillovers, patents and the incentives to

innovate in Japan and the United States. *Research Policy*, 2002, 31(8-9):1349 ~ 1367

7   Cohen, W., Levinthal, D. Absorptive capability: A new perspective on learning and innovation. *Administrative Science Quarterly*, 1990,35:128 ~ 152

8.   Edward Kahn, Patent Mining in a Changing World of Technology and Product Development. *Intellectual Assets Management*, July/ August,2003

9   Gambardella, A., Giuri, P., Luzzi, A. The market for patents in Europe. *Research Policy*, 2007,36(8): 1163 ~ 1183

10   intellectual property bureau in Hunan Province. *Patent Search Handbook in Strategic Emerging Industries*. Beijing: Intellectual Property Publishing House, 2012

11   Intellectual Property Office in Hunan. *Strategic emerging industries Patent Search Guide*. Beijing: Intellectual Property Press, 2013:426 ~ 494

12   J. S. Gans and S. Stern. The Product Market and the Market for Ideas: Commercialization Strategies for Technology Entrepreneurs. *Research Policy*, 2003, 32 (2):333 ~ 350

13   Janghyeok Y, Kwangsoo K. An analysis of property-function based patent networks for strategic R&D

planning in fast-moving industries: The case of silicon-based thin film solar cells. *Expert Systems with Applications*, 2012, 39(9):4409 ~ 7717

14 Jianling Zhang, Guoshun Wang. Energy saving technologies and productive efficiency in the Chinese iron and steel sector. *Energy*. 2008,33(4):525 ~ 537

15 Kaihua Chen, Jianchen Guan. A bibliometric investigation of research performance in emerging nanobio pharmaceuticals. *Journal of Informatics*, 2011, 5 (2): 233 ~ 247

16 Kani, Masayo & Motohashi, Kazuyuki. Understanding the technology market for patents: New insights from a licensing survey of Japanese firms. *Research Policy*, Elsevier, 2012, 41(1): 226 ~ 235

17 Lee Petherbridge, R Polk Wagner. The Federal Circuit and Patentability: An Empirical Assessment of the Law of Obviousness. *Texas Law Review*, 2007, 85(6):7

18 Li Wei and Wang Hongqi: Strategic alliance network cooperation model of new strategic industry. *Learning and Exploration*, 2011 (3):194 ~ 196

19 Li Weiwei. The strategy formulation and implementation of the patent standardization in the new energy automotive industry. *China Science and Technology*

Forum. 2012 (6):62 ~ 68

20　Li Wenhui, Sun Chenguang. The possibility and the path selection to achieve the leap development of the new energy automobile. *Chinese Business*, 2012 (12):372 ~ 373

21　Liang Jun. Research of China's patent licensing value measure. *Electronic intellectual property*, 2011 (5): 52 ~ 55

22　Liu Fudong, Zhu Xuezhong, Wen Jiachun. Study on the patent system oriented to low-carbon develops. *China Soft Science Magazine*, 2011, (7): 25 ~ 30

23　Liu Shumei, Liu Yuping. Analysis of present situation and proposals for development measures of environmental protection industry in China. *Environmental science and management*, 2005, 30(3):11 ~ 12

24　Luan Chunjuan, Wang Xukun, Liu Zeyuan. Comparative study on the patents distributions of Samsung electronics Co., Ltd. and Huawei technologies Co., Ltd., J. *Scientific Management Research*, 2(2008)117 ~ 121

25　Mu Ying. The research of monopoly agreements and Patent cross-licensing agreement. *Technology and Law* , 2013, (4):9 ~ 13

26　Qi Jinmao. Research of new strategic industry

International Cooperation pattern. *Asia-Pacific Economic*, 2011 (6):112 ~ 117

27 R. Polk Wagner, Katherine J. Strandburg. The Obviousness Requirement in the Patent Law. *University of Pennsylvania Law Review*, 2007,155: 96

28 R.W. Rycroft: Does cooperation absorb complexity? Innovation networks and the speed and spread of complex technological innovation. *Technol. Forecasting Soc. Change*, 2007 (7):565 ~ 578

29 Silipo, Damiano B. The Evolution of Cooperation in Patent Races: Theory and Experimental Evidence. *Journal of Economics*, 2005, 85 (1):1 ~ 38. Diagram, 4 Charts, 4 Graphs

30 State Intellectual Property Office (SIPO). The total reports of patents statistical analysis in strategic emerging industries. http://www.sipo.gov.cn/tjxx/, 2014-05-13

31 The planning and development division of state intellectual property office in China. S*ituational analysis report on the patents of the new energy automobile industry*. 2012 (11):1 ~ 16

32 The State Intellectual Property Office of PRC. *The Management Measures of Priority examination of invention patent applications*. 2012

33 Wang Yong, Wang Zhanglin. The patent analysis of the new energy technology in independent brand automotive enterprises. *Automotive Engineers*. 2012 (4):19 ~ 21

34 Xu Guoxiang, Yu Bitao, Li Fushen, Ai Juan. The analysis of patent application for the new energy automobile in China. *The Battery*. 2012 (5):289 ~ 292

35 Xu Ming. The research of patent licensing income in communication industry technical standards. *Science and technology management*, 2012, (11):19 ~ 23

36 Yanghaixia. The opportunities of the new energy vehicles in China. *China Investment*, 2008 (9): 11

37 Yu Jiang, Chen Kaihua. Current situation and challenge of technological innovations in Chinese strategic emerging industries: a patent-bibilometric perspective. *Studies in Science of Science*, 2012, 30 (5): 682 ~ 695

38 Yuan Huazhi, Jian Xiaoping, Yuan Huajian. Research on the competitiveness of the new energy vehicle industry in China. *Science and Technology Management Research*, 2012, (17):42

39 Yu-Shan Chen, Bi-Yu Chen. Utilizing patent analysis to explore the cooperative competition relationship of the two LED companies: Nichia and Osram. *Technological Forecasting & Social Change*, 2005 (78) :

294～302

40 Zhang Man. Analysis of risk aversion of corporate patent licensing. *Business review*, 2012 (5): 54～55

41 Zhang Yangping, Tang Xuan. Development theories of strategic emerging industries and practice experiences for reference: A case study of the energy saving and environmental protection industry in Guangdong province. *Modern Urban Research,* 2012, 27(7): 81～87

42 Zheng Wei. Research on the technology patent of the new energy vehicles. *Automotive Engineering*, 2009 (5):43～45

43 Zhou Ying, Qiu Honghua. A comparative study on green technology patents of American and Japanese automakers as well as its enlightenment. *Journal of Intelligence*, 2010, 29 (2): 21～26

44 操秀英，何建昆. 战略性新兴产业知识产权研究等待破题. 科技日报，2011-04-21

45 董安丹. 美国专利法上之非显著性——历史发展及GRAHAM原则(上). 智慧财产权，1999（10）:80～87

46 甘绍宁. 战略性新兴产业专利技术动向研究. 北京：知识产权出版社，2013

47 郭淑娟，常京萍. 战略性新兴产业知识产权质押融资模式运作及其政策配置. 中国科技论坛，2012

（1）：120～125

48　国家信息中心信息资源开发部．战略性新兴产业2013年发展形势．2014

49　国家信息中心信息资源开发部战略性新兴产业研究小组．2014年一季度战略性新兴产业发展形势调研报告．http://www.sic.gov.cn/News/82/2719.htm, 2014-05-31

50　国家知识产权局．战略性新兴产业发明专利统计分析总报告．http://www.sipo.gov.cn/tjxx/. 2014-06-01

51　国家知识产权局规划发展司．新能源汽车产业专利态势分析报告．专利统计简报，2011（11）：1～16

52　国家知识产权局规划发展司．战略性新兴产业授权发明专利统计报告．专利统计简报，2013（11）：34～35

53　国家知识产权局规划发展司．新能源汽车产业专利态势分析报告，2011（18）

54　韩永进．城市创新经济结构体选择战略性新兴产业路线图研究．见：2010年度京津冀区域协作论坛论文集，2010，295～302

55　湖南省知识产权局．战略性新兴产业专利检索手册．北京:知识产权出版社，2013，426～494

56　贾品荣．培育和发展新兴产业需要知识产权战略．中国经济时报，2010-10-22

57 姜大鹏，顾新．我国战略性新兴产业的现状分析．科技进步与对策，2010（17）：65~70

58 靳茂勤．我国战略性新兴产业国际合作模式初探．亚太经济，2011（6）：46~50

59 李葳，王宏起．战略性新兴产业的战略联盟网络化合作模式．学习与探究，2011（3）：179~181

60 李薇薇．新能源汽车产业的专利标准化战略制定与实施．中国科技论坛，2012（6）：62~68

61 李文辉，孙晨光．实现新能源汽车跨越式发展的可能性和路径选择．中国商界，2010（12）：372~373

62 李文增，王金杰，等．对国内外发展战略性新兴产业的比较研究．见：2010年度京津冀区域协作论坛论文集，2010，313~318

63 李耀新，等．战略产业论．哈尔滨：黑龙江科技出版社，1991:5

64 梁军．中国发明专利许可价值衡量指标研究．电子知识产权，2011（5）：52~55

65 林学军．战略性新兴产业的发展与形成模式研究．中国软科学，2012（2）：26~34

66 吕政．产业政策的制订与战略性产业的选择．北京行政学院学报，2004（4）：28~30

67 栾春娟，王续琨，刘则渊．三星电子公司与华为

技术公司专利布局的比较．科学管理研究，2008
（2）：117~121

68 马德秀．产学研用合作创新推动战略性新兴产业发
展．中国科技产业，2011（1）：16~17

69 毛金生，程文婷．战略性新兴产业知识产权政策初
探．知识产权，2011（9）：63~69

70 毛金生．掌握核心技术知识产权培育战略性新兴产
业．中国高新区，2010（10）：18~20

71 孟海燕．实施知识产权战略是培育和发展战略性新
兴产业的关键．中国发明与专利，2011（9）：17~18

72 芮明杰，赵春明．战略性产业与国有战略控股公司
模式．财经研究，1999（9）：35~39

73 穆颖．垄断协议与专利许可交叉问题研究．科技与
法律，2013（4）：9~13

74 牛立超，祝尔娟．战略性新兴产业发展与主导产业
变迁的关系．发展研究，2011（6）：77~81

75 漆苏，朱雪忠，陈沁．企业自主创新中的专利风险
评价研究．情报杂志，2009（12）：1~4

76 乔永忠，朱雪忠．基于维持时间的发明专利质量实
证研究——以1994年中国专利局授权发明专利为例．
优秀专利调查研究报告集（六）．北京：知识产权出
版社，2010，291~311

77 乔永忠．专利维持时间影响因素研究．科研管理，

2011（7）：143～152

78　宋河发，万劲波，任中保．我国战略性新兴产业内涵特征、产业选择与发展政策研究．科技促进发展，2010（9）：7～13

79　孙国民．警惕战略性新兴产业发展的误区．中国经济问题，2013（3）：45～50

80　孙国民．战略性新兴产业概念界定：一个文献综述．科学管理研究，2014（2）：43～47

81　汤建辉．发展战略性新兴产业亟须知识产权保护．湖北日报，2010-12-11

82　唐宝莲．江苏省环保领域专利开发利用活动分析．江苏科技信息，2005（8）：28～29

83　田力普．知识产权是培育和发展战略性新兴产业的关键．经济日报，2012-05-04

84　万钢．把握全球产业调整机遇培育和发展战略性新兴产业．求是，2010（1）：28～30

85　汪陆洋．重视知识产权战略夯实战略性新兴产业．新材料产业，2011（9）：79～81

86　王新新．战略性新兴产业发展规律及发展对策分析研究．科学管理研究，2011（4）：1～5

87　王永，汪张林．自主品牌汽车企业新能源专利分析．汽车工程师，2011（4）：19～21

88　魏庆华，张新明．粤港澳环保产业专利态势分析与

对策研究. 广东科技, 2003 (7): 74~76

89　温太璞. 发达国家战略性产业政策和贸易政策的理论思考和启示. 商业研究, 2001 (10): 25~27

90　邢红萍, 卫平. 我国战略性新兴产业企业技术创新特征分析——基于全国七省市战略性新兴产业企业问卷调查. 中国科技论坛, 2013 (7): 66~73

91　徐国详, 余碧涛, 李福燊, 艾娟. 我国新能源汽车领域专利申请情况分析. 电池, 2012 (5): 289~292

92　徐明. 通信产业技术标准中专利许可的收益研究. 科学与科学技术管理, 2012 (5): 19~23

93　薛澜, 林泽梁, 梁正, 等. 世界战略性新兴产业的发展趋势对我国的启示. 中国软科学, 2013 (5): 18~27

94　杨海霞. 新能源汽车的中国机遇. 中国投资, 2008-09-11

95　余江, 陈凯华. 提升知识产权战略能力, 推动战略性新兴产业发展. 科技促进发展, 2011 (3): 48~51

96　余江, 陈凯华. 中国战略性新兴产业的技术创新现状与挑战——基于专利文献计量的角度. 科学学研究, 2012 (5): 682~695

97　袁华智, 塞小平, 袁华剑. 我国新能源汽车产业竞争力研究. 科技管理研究, 2012 (17): 42

98　张曼．企业专利许可风险的规避探析．商业经济评论，2012（5）：54～55

99　张鹏．战略性新兴产业发展的知识产权制度回应．中国发明与专利，2011（9）：19～23

100　张延平，汤萱．战略性新兴产业发展理论分析与实践经验借鉴——以广东省节能环保产业为例．现代城市研究，2012（7）：81～87

101　赵玉林，张倩男．湖北省战略性主导产业的选择研究．中南财经政法大学学报，2007（2）：30～35

102　郑江淮．理解战略性新兴产业的发展：概念、可能的市场失灵与发展定位．上海金融学院学报，2010（4）：5～10

103　郑薇．新能源汽车的技术专利研究．汽车技术，2009（5）：43～45

104　中国国务院．"十二五"国家战略性新型产业发展规划，2010

105　中国国务院．"十二五"节能环保产业发展规划，2010

106　朱瑞博，刘芸．战略性新兴产业的培育及其自主创新．重庆社会科学，2011（2）：45～53

107　朱瑞博．中国战略性新兴产业培育及其政策取向．改革，2010（3）：19～28

108　朱迎春．政府在发展战略性新兴产业中的作用．中国科技论坛，2011（1）：20～24

附录：已发表的相关国际会议论文

I. Research on the Patent Licensing of the New Generation Information Technology Industry in China*

Abstract: With the development of the new generation of information technology industry, the cooperation mode of enterprises becomes more and more complicated. A research on the technological cooperation is of a significance based on a perspective of patent licensing. By analyzing the patent licensing data of Huawei, Lenovo, ZTE and Datang in the new generation information technology industry in China, we can draw the following conclusions: the patent licensing amount of three companies show the wave declining trend yearly; there are an obvious difference in the distributions of the product patent, the process patent, the product and process patent of patent licensing in the different enterprises; there are an obvious difference in the positions of patent licensing in the different enterprises.

Keywords: new generation, information technology, patent licensing

1. Introduction

The new generation information technology industry is one of the

*   Yongzhong Qiao, Siwen Liu. Research on the Patent Licensing of the New Generation Information Technology Industry in China. *Applied Mechanics and Materials*. 2014, (536-537): 1733-1736.

seven major strategic emerging industries in China. **❶** As a mode of technological cooperation in enterprises, patent licensing also more and more are adapted by enterprises. The research results of the patent cooperation are mostly about the patent cooperation of countries under the economic globalization environment, **❷** Network co-op **❸** and the speed and dissemination of the network technology innovation. **❹** These researches of patent licensing mainly concentrated on the domains of the patent licensing evaluation index, **❺** the development of the cooperation of pattern patent race. **❻** and how to avoid the patent licensing risk of enterprises, **❼** etc. Some scholars also studied the technical standards of the patent licensing revenue in communications industry, **❽**

---

❶ The State Council of the PRC., *The development plans of "12th five-year" for the national strategic emerging industries* (2010).In Chinese.

❷ Qi Jinmao, Research of new strategic industry International Cooperation pattern, *Asia—Pacific Economic,* 2011 (6):112-117. In Chinese.

❸ li Wei and Wang Hongqi, Strategic alliance network cooperation model of new strategic industry, *Learning and Exploration,* 2011 (3):194-196. In Chinese.

❹ R.W. Rycroft, Does cooperation absorb complexity? Innovation networks and the speed and spread of complex technological innovation, Technol, *Forecasting Soc. Change,* 2007 (7):565-578.

❺ Liang Jun, research of China's patent licensing value measure, *Electronic intellectual property*, 2011 (5): 52-55. In Chinese.

❻ Silipo, Damiano B, The Evolution of Cooperation in Patent Races: Theory and Experimental Evidence, *Journal of Economics*, 2005, 85 (1):1-38. Diagram, 4 Charts, 4 Graphs.

❼ Zhang Man, Analysis of risk aversion of corporate patent licensing, *Business review*, 2012 (5): 54-55. In Chinese.

❽ Xu Ming, The research of patent licensing income in communication industry technical standards, *Science and technology management*, 2012, (11):19-23. In Chinese.

the problem of monopoly agreements and the patent cross-licensing.❶ However, there are a few of works to analyzing the situation of enterprise cooperation from the patent licensing cases in the particular industry. Therefore, this paper will analyze the patent licensing data of the enterprises cooperation progress in the new generation information technology industry, then draw some conclusions for improve the using ability of intellectual property of enterprises and promote the development of the new generation information technology industry.

2. Data Sources and Research Methods

In this paper, the patent licensing data come from the record information of the patent licensing contract and the service platform of patent information published by State Intellectual Property Office in China (SIPO) (http://search.cnipr.com/). The specific methods are input "2009-2013" in the publication date of legal status bar, input "licensing" in legal status bar, then according to these result to retrieve the specific information of the new generation of information technology industry.

According to the " the Top 100 Electronic Information enterprises in China in 2012" announced by the Ministry of Industry and Information Technology in China, and referencing the main business direction of enterprises,

---

❶ Mu Ying, The research of monopoly agreements and Patent cross-licensing agreement, *Technology and Law* , 2013, (4):9-13. In Chinese.

select Huawei Technologies Co., Ltd. (abbreviation "Huawei"), Lenovo Mobile Communication Technology Co., Company (abbreviation "Lenovo"), ZTE Corporation (abbreviation "ZTE") and Datang Telecom Technology Group (abbreviation "Datang") from the new generation of information technology industry as representatives enterprises, analyze the trends of patent licensing volume, the licenses objects, and study the patent cooperation of enterprises in the new generation information technology industry.

3. Data Analysis

3.1 The developing trends of patent licensing in four representative enterprises

From the number of patent licensing of Huawei, Lenovo, ZTE and Datang (Table 1), the following two trends could be found: first, the patent licensing number show the wavy declining trend in three companies, except Lenovo; second, the patent licensing number is increasing yearly in Lenovo. In particular Lenovo had no the patent licensing records in 2009 and 2010, there is a small amount of patent licensing began to appear gradually in 2011, and then surged in 2013.

Table 1 The number distribution of patent licensing of four representative enterprises

	2009	2010	2011	2012	2013
Huawei	23	6	10	1	0
ZTE	47	3	13	5	1
Lenovo	0	0	5	15	68
Datang	9	4	7	1	2

The quantity surging of patent licensing is related to the technical cooperation of Lenovo with the Dolby Company in 2013. According to the record information, almost all patent licensing of Lenovo are from the Dolby Laboratories. The cooperation of the Dolby and Lenovo launched in the strong entertainment function and theater audio experience of PC products in 2005, but the true cooperation of patent licensing between the Dolby Laboratories and Lenovo began in June 2012. After that, Lenovo used the fourth generation advanced technology of Dolby home theater or the second generation of Dolby PC audio technology on products such as ThinkPad, Think Centre, Idea Pa and Idea Centre, so as to make the surge of patent licensing in Lenovo in 2013.

3.2 The distributions of the patent types to licensing in four representative enterprises

Except ZTE have five design patents in patent licensing, patent licensing of other three enterprises are invention patent or utility model patent. In other perspective, the patent types to licensing can be dividing into the product patent, the process patent, and the product and process patent. The distributions of the patent types to licensing of four representative enterprises are very different (Table 2).

Table 2 The distributions of patent types to licensing of four representative enterprises

	Huawei	Lenovo	ZTE	Datang
The product and process patent	22	27	23	11
The process patent	11	18	23	8
The product patent	7	43	23	4

From table 2, we can draw a feature of the distributions of the patent types to licensing of four representative enterprises, namely, the patent types to licensing of Huawei and Datang involve the product patent and the process patent mainly, the patent type to licensing of Lenovo involves the product patent mainly, and the proportion of the patent types to licensing of ZTE is a little different, which involve the product patent, the process patent, and the product and process patent. The main reasons are related to the business distribution of these enterprises. The business of Huawei include the products and solutions covering the mobile, the broadband, the IP, the optical network, the telecommunication value-added services and terminals and so on, which are committed to providing full IP integration solution, so the process patent are more than the product patent in Huawei. Lenovo, the leadership of global PC market enterprises, mainly produces the desktop computers, the servers, the laptop computer, the printer, the PDA, the motherboard, the mobile phones and other goods, so the type of patent licensing more focus on the product patent. ZTE is the global leader of the solutions providers of integrated communications, and the world fourth largest mobile phone manufacturers, so the proportion of two business pieces is equal. This reflects that the proportion of the product patent and the process patent of patent licensing are equal too; Datang's main business domain includes the communication terminal industry and the coordination with the communication terminal applications and services industry, so the content of the patent licensing also involves the product patent and the process patent. This shows that the patent types to licensing of enterprise are related with their main business domain.

3.3 The licensor or licensee distribution of patent licensing in four representative enterprises

According to the licensor or licensee distribution of patent licensing in four representative enterprises (Table 3), we can find the similarities and differences between the models of licensing patents.

Table 3 The licensors or licensees distribution of patent licensing in four representative enterprises

	Huawei	Lenovo	ZTE	Datang
Licensor	40	3	67	30
Licensee	0	85	2	0

Huawei and Datang all are licensors in their patent licensing. The licensees of patent licensing is not fixed in Huawei, most of which are companies of Guangdong province. Huawei is the second largest communication equipment supplier and the third largest smart phone manufacturer in the world, and the domestic amount of patent licensing reduced yearly. The situations of patent licensing in Datang mostly are the patent licensing within the enterprise, which is inseparable with the complex internal structure in Datang. All of patent licensing in Datang are subordinate enterprises of the Datang group, which mainly include the Xi 'an Datang Telecom Co., Ltd, the Datang Mobile Communication Equipment Co., Ltd, the Datang Microelectronics Technology Co., Ltd, the Datang Telecom Technology Co., Ltd, Telecommunications Institute of Science and Technology and Datang Microelectronics Technology Co., Ltd. The licensees are also inside companies of the Datang group, including the Datang Telecom Technical Services (Tianjin) Co., Ltd, the Datang Telecom Communication Terminal Manufacturing (Tianjin) Co., Ltd, the Datang Telecom Technology Industry Holding Co., Ltd, and the Fourth Telecommunications Institute of Science and Technology, in addition to the licensing patents in Datang have 2 pieces of other companies, they are the Shanghai Feili Communications Technology Industrial Company and Guangzhou Mingsen Mechanical and Electrical Equipment Co., Ltd.

Most of licensing patents in ZTE are licensing others to use, including 81% of the total amount of licensing patents are the permission to internal company, and the other companies accounted for only 19% of licensing patents. The licensor of licensing patents in ZTE all are ZTE co., LTD, except 2 pieces of licensing patents are licensed for the Italian interest thinking co., LTD. Therefore, the internal licensing type of patents in ZTE is more important than that of licensing patents with other enterprise.

However, the licensors or licensees distribution of patent licensing of Lenovo are very different with that of other enterprises. Three pieces patents are licensed the Lenovo Mobile Communication Technology Co., Ltd, Lenovo Mobile Communications Software (Wuhan) Co., Ltd. The rest of the 85 pieces patents licensed to use of others, and licensees are fixed to the Dolby Laboratories licensing Company and the Dolby International Company, including 33 pieces are the Dolby Laboratories Licensing Company and the Dolby International Companies, which licensed the Lenovo Mobile Communication Technology Co., Ltd, 52 pieces is the Dolby Laboratories Licensing Company and the Dolby International Company Licensed Lenovo (Beijing) Co., Ltd. The Dolby Laboratories Licensing Company and the Dolby International Company mainly invented the noise reduction technology and the voice compression coding technology, etc., in accordance with the proportion of products patent in Lenovo.

4. Conclusions

Based on the perspective of patent licensing to analyzing the technology cooperation is of significance. Through the empirical analysis of patent licensing in four representative enterprises of the new generation of information industry in China in 2009 ~ 2013,we can draw the following five conclusions: first, the amount of patent licensing shows the wave downward trend in the three companies; second, the patent types to licensing of Huawei and ZTE are major in the product and process patent, the patent type to licensing of Lenovo is major in the product patent, and the proportion of the patent types to licensing of ZTE is a few difference; third, most of patent licensing in ZTE are the enterprise internal licenses; Fourth, the patent licensors in Lenovo and Datang are relatively fixed; Fifth, the licensees of patent in the Huawei are not fixed.

II. Research on the Technical Fields Distribution of Patents Licensing of Chinese Firms in the Next-Generation Information Technology Industry*

Abstract: By analyzing the patents licensing data of Huawei, Lenovo, ZTE and Datang in the next-generation information technology industry in China, the following conclusions can be drawn: Huawei and Lenovo's technical fields of patents licensing respectively concentrate on the field of the manufacture of assemblages of electrical components, the fields of the speech analysis or synthesis, the speech recognition, the speech or voice processing and the speech or audio coding or decoding, ZTE and Datang's technical field of patents licensing both concentrate on field of the selecting.

Keywords: technical field, patent licensing, the next-generation information technology industry

1. Introduction

The next-generation information technology industry is one of the seven major strategic emerging industries in

---

* Yongzhong Qiao, Siwen Liu. Research on the Technical Fields Distribution of Patents Licensing of Chinese Firms in the Next-Generation Information Technology Industry, *Applied Mechanics and Materials*, 2014, (530-531):1142-1145.

China.[1] With the development of the next-generation of information technology industry, the cooperation mode of patents in enterprises become more complicated. Although the technology market for patents is far from perfect because of high transaction costs and information asymmetry between potential licensors and licensees,[2] and a large number of firms do not license although they are willing to do so because such patents are less appealing.[3] In addition, the high transaction costs associated with the market for patents hinder the licensing of even appealing patents.[4] However, in the information technological industry, patents are perceived as a relatively effective tool of appropriating rents from technological innovation[5] and the licensing propensity in such industries may be higher than in others. In addition, firm size matters as well because the rent dissipation effect of licensing, due to increased competition in the product market, is smaller for small and medium-sized enterprises (SMEs)

---

[1] The State Council of the PRC. The Development plans of "12th five-year" for the national strategic emerging industries (2010). In Chinese.

[2] J. S. Gans and S. Stern, The Product Market and the Market for Ideas: Commercialization Strategies for Technology Entrepreneurs, *Research Policy*, 2003, 32(2):333-350.

[3] Gambardella, A., Giuri, P., Luzzi, A. The market for patents in Europe. *Research Policy*, 2007,36(8):1163-1183.

[4] Kani, Masayo & Motohashi, Kazuyuki. Understanding the technology market for patents: New insights from a licensing survey of Japanese firms, *Research Policy, Elsevier*, 2012, 41(1): 226-235.

[5] Cohen, W. M., Goto, A., Nagata, A., Nelson, R. R., & Walsh, J. P. R&D spillovers, patents and the incentives to innovate in Japan and the United States. *Research Policy*, 2002, 31(8-9):1349-1367.

that do not have a significant presence in the product market.❶
At same time, according to the absorptive capacity theory, a
potential licensee is typically a large firm that can conduct
substantial in-house complementary R&D.❷ Therefore, as
a mode of technological cooperation in enterprises, patents
licensing more and more are adapted by enterprises. In
China, the works of patents licensing mainly concentrated on
the domains of the patents licensing evaluation index,❸ the
development of the cooperation of pattern patent race ❹ and
how to avoid the patents licensing risk of enterprises.
However, there are a few of works to analyzing the situation
of enterprises cooperation from patents licensing cases in the
particular industry. For this purposes, this paper main study
the technical fields distribution of patents licensing of Chinese
large firms in the next-generation information technology
industry.

2. Data Sources and Research Methods

In this paper, the patents licensing data come from the
record information of patents licensing contracts and the

---

❶　Arora, A., Fosfuri, A. Licensing the market for technology, *Journal of Economic
Behavior & Organization*, 2003, (52): 277-295.

❷　Cohen, W., Levinthal, D. Absorptive capability: A new perspective on learning
and innovation. *Administrative Science Quarterly*, 1990,35:128-152.

❸　Liang Jun: research of China's patent licensing value measure. *Electronic
intellectual property*, 2011, (5): 52-55. In Chinese.

❹　Silipo, Damiano B. The Evolution of Cooperation in Patent Races: Theory and
Experimental Evidence, *Journal of Economics*, 2005, 85 (1):1-38. Diagram, 4 Charts, 4
Graphs.

service platform of patent information published by State Intellectual Property Office in China (SIPO) (http://search. cnipr.com/).The specific methods are input "2009 ~ 2013" in the publication date of legal status bar, and input "licensing" in the legal status bar, then according to these results to retrieve the specific information of the International Patent Classification (IPC) of patents licensing in the next-generation of information technology industry. ❶

According to the " the top 100 electronic information enterprises in China in 2012" announced by the Ministry of Industry and Information Technology in China, and referencing the main business direction of enterprises, select Huawei Technologies Co., Ltd. (abbreviation "Huawei"), Lenovo Mobile Communication Technology Co., Ltd. (abbreviation "Lenovo"), ZTE Corporation (abbreviation "ZTE") and Datang Telecom Technology Group (abbreviation "Datang") from the next-generation of information technology industry as representative enterprises.

3. Data Analysis

The IPC provides for a hierarchical system of language independent symbols for the classification of patents according to the different areas of technology to which they pertain. The IPC divides technology into eight sections with approximately 70,000 subdivisions. Each subdivision has a

---

❶ Intellectual Property Office in Hunan Province: *Strategic emerging industries Patent Search Guide*. Intellectual Property Press, 2013:426-494. In Chinese.

symbol consisting of Arabic numerals and letters of the Latin alphabet. The main NGIT items include: the next-generation mobile communications, the next-generation core Internet equipment, the convergence of Telecom/ Cable TV/ Internet networks, the Cloud Computing, etc. According to the IPC symbol, by analyzing the distributions of technical fields of patents licensing, we can master the output and demand level of technologies in four representative enterprises.

3.1 The Distribution of the Sections of Technical Fields of Patents Licensing

According to the IPC symbol and the distribution of the sections of technical fields of patents licensing in four enterprises (Table 1),❶ the technical fields of patents licensing of four enterprises in the new generation of information technology industry mainly distributed in G (physics) section and H (electricity) section, in a small amount of B (performing operations, transporting) section and C (chemistry and metallurgy) section. In H (electricity) section, ZTE's the number of patents licensing is the largest, other firms' number of patents licensing are a few differences. In G (physics), Lenovo's the number of patents licensing is the largest; Huawei and ZYE' number of patents licensing are a few

---

❶ The International Patent Classification represents the whole body of knowledge which may be regarded as proper to the field of patents for invention, divided into eight sections. Sections are the highest level of hierarchy of the classification.

differences; Datang's the number of patents licensing is the lowest, which is as same as its number of patents licensing in C (chemistry and metallurgy) section.

Table 1 The distribution of the sections of technical fields of patents licensing in four enterprises

	H	G	C	B
Huawei	50	26	1	1
Lenovo	55	52	0	0
ZTE	112	22	0	0
Datang	41	6	6	0

3.2 The Distribution of the Classes of Technical Fields of Patents Licensing

Each section is subdivided into classes which are the second hierarchical level of the classification. The classes distribution of the technical fields of patents licensing in four enterprises (Table 2) shows that the classes distribution of patents licensing are mainly concentrated on H04 (electrical communication technology) class in Lenovo, ZTE and Datang, however, the distribution of patents licensing in Huawei are more dispersed. Specifically, the distribution of this class has following principle features.

Table 2 The distribution of the classes of technical fields of patents licensing in four enterprises

	Huawei	Lenovo	ZTE	Datang
The basic electrical components（H01）	8	0	3	0
The generation, substation and distribution of power（H02）	7	0	4	0
The basic electronic circuit（H03）	1	20	3	1
The electrical communication technology（H04）	15	35	102	40
The other categories not included power technology（H05）	17	0	0	0
The measurement; testing（G01）	11	0	2	3
The control; regulation（G05）	1	0	2	0
The calculation; projections; count（G06）	13	9	14	2
The signal device（G08）	2	0	0	0
The instruments; acoustic（G10）	40	0	3	1
The information storage（G11）	3	0	0	0
The horology（G04）	0	0	1	0

First of all, the distribution of the technical fields of patents licensing in Huawei is relatively scattered, mainly distributed on the fields of G10（instrument and acoustics）class, H05（other categories not included power technology）class and H04（electrical communication technology）class. Second, the distribution of the technical fields of patents licensing are relatively concentrated in Lenovo, ZTE and

Datang. The distribution of the technical fields of patents licensing in Lenovo is mainly distributed on H04 (electrical communication technology) class and H03 (basic electronic circuit field) class; The distribution of the technical fields of patents licensing in ZTE focuses on H04 (electrical communication technology) class and G06 (calculation, projections and count) class and a small amount of patents licensing distributed on H02 (generation, substation and distribution of power) class, H01 (basic electrical components) class, H03 (basic electronic circuit) class, and G10 (instruments, acoustic) class; The distribution of the technical fields of patents licensing in Datang mainly concentrated on H04 (electrinical communication technology) class, and a small amount of patents licensing distributed in G01 (measurement and testing) class.

3.3 The Distribution of the Subclasses of Technical Fields of Patents Licensing

Each class comprises one or more subclasses which are the third hierarchical level of the Classification. Table 3 shows the main distributions of the sub-classes of technical fields of patents licensing in four representative enterprises.

Table 3 The subclasses of technical fields of patents licensing in four representative enterprises

Huawei	H01B	H01L	H02H	H04B	H04L	H05K	G01R	G06F	G06Q	G08G
	3❶	4	6	4	11	17	11	12	2	2
Lenovo	H03G	H03M	H04B	H04N	H04R	H04S	G06F	G10K	G10L	G11B
	13	7	5	6	6	16	7	4	36	3
ZTE	H02H	H02J	H03M	H04B	H04J	H04L	H04M	H04N	H04Q	G06F
	2	2	2	11	6	16	10	4	35	14
Datang	H04B	H04L	H04M	H04Q	H04W	G01S	G06F	G10L	B65D	
	4	12	6	14	2	3	2	2	3	

From Table 3, the following key features can be found. In Huawei, the subclasses of technical fields of patents licensing mainly distribute on H05K (printed circuits, casings or constructional details of electric apparatus, manufacture of assemblages of electrical components) subclass; G06F (electric digital data processing) subclass; G01R (measuring electric variables; measuring magnetic variables) subclass; and H04L (transmission of digital information). In Lenovo, the subclasses of the technical fields of patents licensing mainly distribute on G10L (speech analysis or synthesis, speech recognition, speech or voice processing, speech or audio coding or decoding) subclass; H04S (stereophonic systems) subclass; H03G (control of amplification). In ZTE, the subclasses of technical fields of patents licensing mainly distribute on H04Q (selecting) subclass; G06F (electric digital data processing) subclass; H04L (transmission of

---

❶ The numbers below the subclass symbols are the amount of patents licensing in the technical field.

digital information) subclass; H04B (transmission) subclass; and H04M (telephonic communication). In Datang, the subclasses of technical fields of patents licensing mainly distribute on H04Q (selecting) subclass; H04L (transmission of digital information) subclass; and H04M (telephonic communication) subclass.

4. Conclusion

A research on the technological cooperation is of a great significance based on a perspective of patents licensing. Through the empirical analysis of the distribution of technical fields of patents licensing in four representative enterprises of the new generation of information industry in China in 2009 ~ 2013, we can draw the following conclusions: in the sections of technical field, the technical fields of four firms mainly distributed on physics section and electricity section; in the classes of technical field, Huawei's technical fields of patents licensing is relatively scattered, other three firms' technical fields of patents licensing are mainly concentrate on the electrical communication technical field; in the subclasses of technical field, Huawei and Lenovo's technical fields of patents licensing respectively concentrate on the field of the manufacture of assemblages of electrical components, the fields of the speech analysis or synthesis, the speech recognition, the speech or voice processing and the speech or audio coding or decoding, ZTE and Datang's technical fields of patents licensing both concentrate on the field of selecting.

III. Research on the Granted Patent Distribution of the Energy-saving and Environmental Protection Industry in China[*]

Abstract: By analyzing the granted patents distribution of the energy-saving and environmental protection industry in China from 2008 to 2013, the conclusion can be reached: firstly, technological innovations of the energy-saving industry are focused on the environmentally air-conditioning and heat pump technical field, and technological innovations of the resources recycling industry is mainly concentrated on the food waste treatment and comprehensive utilization technical field and the urban sewage sludge recycling technical field, and technological innovations of the environmental management industry is highly focused on the high concentration organic wastewater control technical field; secondly, the granted patents distributions of the key strategic technical fields are unbalanced, of which the granted patents of the environmental management industry have the largest share; thirdly, the domestic granted patents distributions are basically similar to that of foreign granted patents in the energy-saving and environmental protection industry in China, but the domestic granted patents numbers are more than the foreign granted patents numbers.

---

[*] Yongzhong Qiao, Qi Liang. Research on the Granted Patent Distribution of the Energy-saving and Environmental Protection Industry in China. The thirteenth Wuhan international Conference on E-Business- Knowledge Management and Business Intelligence. 2014, 221-228.

Keywords: energy-saving, environmental protection, granted patent, distribution

1. Introduction

With the severity of the global environmental issues and the shortage of energy resources, it is important to research on the granted patents distributions of the energy-saving and environmental protection technical fields for the development of related industry. The energy-saving and environmental protection industry is one of seven strategic emerging industries in China[1] and it is also one of major industry domains of the Twelfth Five-Year Development Plan in China. The development of the energy-saving and environmental protection industry is of great importance to ease the pressure on traditional energy consumption, foster the new economic growth point and develop the emerging industries.

The development of the energy-saving and environmental protection industry is inseparable from technological innovation. Patent is one of the most reliable measures of the most direct indicators of technological innovation,[2] which would reflect the latest trends of researches in the industry and make companies develop their own technological

---

[1] The State Council of PRC. (2010). Development plans of "12th five-year" for the national strategic emerging industries.

[2] Janghyeok Y, Kwangsoo K. (2012). An analysis of property-function based patent networks for strategic R&D planning in fast-moving industries: The case of silicon-based thin film solar cells. *Expert Systems with Applications*, 39(9):4409-7717.

strategies. [1] The patent system may improve the green technological innovation capability through a continuous cycle process: technological exploitation – protection – utilization – improvement – protection – utilization.[2] In 2012, the patent applications of the low-carbon technology and the energy-saving technology having been advanced examined by State Intellectual Property Office in China (SIPO).[3] This system is conducive to promote the industrial management of the energy-saving technology, which will further promote innovations in the energy-saving and environmental protection industry.[4]

Researches on the energy-saving and environmental protection industry have attracted more and more scholars' attention in home and abroad, because China ranked it as one of strategic emerging industries in 2010. Lots of works have done in the existing researches on the relative field of the industry, such as trends and development, strategies and measures, experience and creation, etc. Though plenty of results of the study have been carried on, most researches are based on the qualitative analysis from the macro perspective,

---

[1]　Brent B. A, Walter G. P. (2007). The influence of patent protection on firm innovation investment in manufacturing industries. *Journal of International Management*, 13 (2):91–109.

[2]　Liu Fudong, Zhu Xuezhong, Wen Jiachun. (2011). Study on the patent system oriented to low-carbon develops. *China Soft Science Magazine*, (7): 25–30. (in Chinese)

[3]　The State Intellectual Property Office of PRC. (2012). *The Management Measures of Priority examination of invention patent applications.* (in Chinese)

[4]　Bingbin Lu. (2013). Expedited patent examination for green inventions: Developing countries policy choice. *Energy Policy*, 61(10): 1529–1538.

lacking of quantitative and empirical research on patent issues of the energy-saving and environmental protection industry. The quantitative and empirical analysis of patents is in favor of clearing the difference in innovation ability and the technological gap of between domestic and foreign technical fields. [1] In that way, we would figure out more effective strategies to further develop the industry of China.

A developing trend of patents is one of an important indicator of industrial development, and the use of patent indicators to quantitative analysis the level of industrial technology and the innovation capability is a new research trend.[2] It is the most common method to analyze the steady exponential growth characteristics of the patent document of related industrial technologies which can determine technological innovation activities in the industry.[3][4] In order to clarify the technological development characteristics of the energy-saving and environmental protection industry and promote the industry development in China, we analyzed quantitatively

---

[1] Yu Jiang, Chen Kaihua. (2012). Current situation and challenge of technological innovations in Chinese strategic emerging industries: a patent-bibilometric perspective. *Studies in Science of Science*, 30 (5): 682-695. (in Chinese)

[2] Zhou Ying, Qiu Honghua. (2010). A comparative study on green technology patents of American and Japanese automakers as well as its enlightenment. *Journal of Intelligence*, 29 (2): 21-26. (in Chinese)

[3] Yu Jiang, Chen Kaihua. (2012). Current situation and challenge of technological innovations in Chinese strategic emerging industries: a patent-bibilometric perspective. *Studies in Science of Science*, 30 (5): 682-695. (in Chinese)

[4] Kaihua Chen, Jianchen Guan. (2011). A bibliometric investigation of research performance in emerging nanobio pharmaceuticals. *Journal of Informatics*, 5 (2): 233-247.

the industry development status and trends of the energy-saving and environmental protection industry by the method of patent-bibliometric.

2. Data Source and Industry Classification

In this article, the granted patents statistics is searched by IPC (International Patent Classification) in the platform of patent-searching system of Patent Star (http://searchtel. patentstar.com.cn/) from 2008 to 2013; and the information of the granted patents of the energy-saving and environmental protection industry is analyzed; then the development trends and patent problems in the industry in China are exposed.

The energy-saving and environmental protection industry is divided into the energy-saving industry, the resources recycling industry and the environmental management industry. Their main technical areas involved the International Patent Classification (IPC) symbols are based on the "Patent Search Handbook in Strategic Emerging Industries". ❶

---

❶ Zhang Yang Ping, Tang Xuan (2012) Development theorves of strateglc emerglyindustries and practice expervences for reference: A case study of the energy saning and environmental tection industry in Guangdong province Modern Urban Research, 27(7): 81-87. (in Chinese)

3. The Granted Patents Distribution of the Energy-Saving and Environmental Protection Industry

3.1 The overall features of the granted patents

3.1.1 The distribution of granted patents in three sub-industries

Based on the statistics of granted patents in nearly six years of the energy-saving and environmental protection industry in China, we can draw some features of the development status and trends of patented technology in energy-saving, resources recycling and environmental management industries.

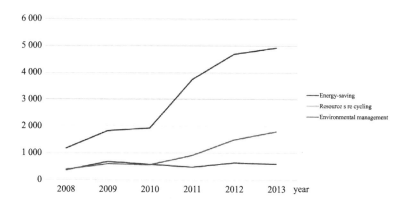

Figure 1 The trends of granted patents in the energy-saving and environmental protection industries

Figure 1 shows the trends of granted patents of the energy-saving and environmental protection industry in China from 2008 to 2013. We could find that the characteristics of granted patents in the industry. Firstly, the granted patent numbers of three technical fields have been increasing during the period of 2008 ~ 2013, but the growth rates were different. The growth rate of the granted patent number of the environmental management industry is the sharpest, and the growth rate of the granted patent number of the energy-saving industry is the lowest. Secondly, the growth rates of the granted patents are different in different periods in three technical fields. The growth rates were lower in three technical fields during 2008 ~ 2010. The growth rate of granted patents of environmental management industry was the highest, but the growth rate of granted patents of the resource recycling industry was low during 2010 ~ 2012. The granted patents numbers of the energy-saving industry and the environmental management industry slightly decreased during 2012 ~ 2013. Apparently, the innovation capability of the environment management industry was significantly stronger than that of the other two industries in this period.

3.1.2 The domestic and foreign granted patents distributions of in the tree technical fields

The domestic and foreign patents distributions of the three technical fields are shown in figure 2 and these patents were granted by State Intellectual Property Office of the PRC (SIPO) from 2008 to 2013. Two characteristics can be found from figure 2: firstly, the domestic granted patents are dominant in the three technical fields of the energy-saving and environmental protection industry in China. There are obvious advantages in the three technical domains for domestic patentees, and foreign patentees are not threats to the related industrial development in China. Secondly, there are different technical advantages degrees in various technologies for the holders of domestic granted patents. The patents advantages of the environmental management industry are the most obvious, slightly followed by the resources recycling industry, and the energy-saving industry is the weakest.

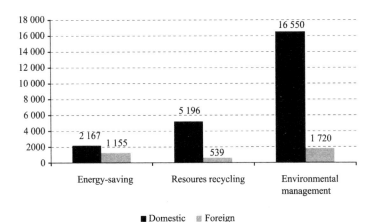

Figure 2 The domestic and foreign granted patents distributions of three fields

4. The Granted Patents Distributions of the Energy-Saving Industry

The technical field of the energy-saving industry includes the industrial boiler design and manufacturing technology (F22B9/00-F22B9/18, F22B27/00-F22B27/16, and F22B29/00-F22B29/12), the waste heat and energy utilization technology (F27D17/00) and the environmentally air conditioning and heat pump technology (F24F1/00-F24F1/04, F24F3/00-F24F3/16, F24F5/00, F25B30/00-F25B30/06).

4.1 The granted patents distribution of main technologies in the energy-saving industry

As shown in Figure 3, inventions in the energy-saving industry mainly concentrated on the environmentally air-conditioning and heat pump technology. There are 2 899 granted patents in this technical field, which are accounted for 87.3% in all granted patents in the industry, and there are 388 granted patents in the technical field of the waste heat and energy utilization. The industrial boiler design and manufacturing technology only get 35 granted patents in the past six years, which is the least in the three technical fields in the energy-saving industry.

From Figure 3, we could draw conclusion: firstly, there is serious imbalance of the granted patents distribution in the energy-saving industry from 2008 to 2013. It primarily focused on the environmentally air-conditioning and heat pump technology, while the innovative capabilities of other two technologies need to enhance; secondly, the competition of the environmentally air-conditioning and heat pump technology will be more acute in the future.

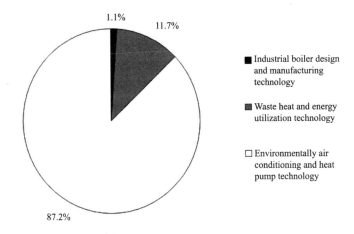

1.1%   11.7%

■ Industrial boiler design and manufacturing technology

■ Waste heat and energy utilization technology

☐ Environmentally air conditioning and heat pump technology

87.2%

Figure 3 The granted patents distribution of main fields of the energy-saving industry

4.2 The domestic and foreign granted patents distributions of the energy-saving industry

The domestic and foreign granted patents distribution of major technical fields in the energy-saving industry (Figure 4) can be found two features. Firstly, there are generally consistent on the domestic and foreign granted patents distributions in the energy-saving industry. The granted patents distributions of both extremely focusing on the environmentally air-conditioning and heat pump technology, and there are relatively small proportions in the waste heat and energy utilization technology and the industrial boiler design and manufacture technology. Secondly, the domestic granted patents amount is absolutely more than that of foreign granted patents in various technical fields. But the gap multiples of domestic and foreign granted patents are not identical. The number of domestic granted patents almost is seven times that of foreign granted patents in the waste heat and energy utilization technology, and is less than doubled in other two technical fields. This shows that the distributions of domestic and foreign granted patents are basically focus on main technical fields in energy-saving industry, however, the domestic granted patents of the waste heat and energy utilization technology has more advantages in China.

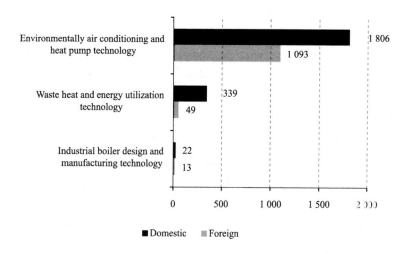

Figure 4 The domestic and foreign granted patents distributions of major fields in energy-saving industry

5. The Granted Patents Distributions of the Resources Recycling Industry

The technologies of the resources recycling industry

include the low-grade metal ore recycling technology (B03B7/00, B03B9/06, B03D1/00-B03D1/26), the comprehensive utilization of desulfurization gypsum technology (C04B7/04, C04B11/00-C04B11/30, C04B28/14-C04B28/16), the comprehensive utilization of coal gangue technology(C04B18/04-C04B18/12, C10L5/48), the food waste treatment and comprehensive utilization technology (B09B1/00, B09B3/00, A23K1/10), the waste material dismantling and sorting processing technology (B29B17/00-B29B17/02, H01M6/25, H01M10/54, H01J9/52), the key re-creation technology (C05F9/00-C05F9/04, B22F8/00), the urban sewage sludge recycling technology (C02F11/00-C02F11/02, C05F7/00-C05F7/04).

5.1 The granted patents distribution of the main fields in the resources recycling industry

The features of the granted patents distribution of the main technologies in the resources recycling industry in China from 2008 to 2013 (Figure 5) are as follows: Firstly, the granted patents of the resource recycling industry mainly focused on the food waste treatment and comprehensive utilization technology and the urban sewage sludge recycling technology, which are more related to human's daily living. Secondly, they are relatively uniform for the granted patents distributions of the low-grade metal ore recycling technology, the comprehensive utilization of desulfurization gypsum technology, and the comprehensive utilization of coal gangue technology. Thirdly, their granted patents amounts of the waste material dismantling and sorting processing technology and the key re-creation technology are lower, and their roles are weaker in the resource recycling industry.

Therefore, the technological innovational capacity of the food waste treatment and comprehensive utilization technology and the urban sewage sludge recycling technology are obviously leading the industrial development, while the technological innovational capacity of the waste material dismantling and sorting processing technology and the key re-creation are relatively weak in the resources recycling industry in China.

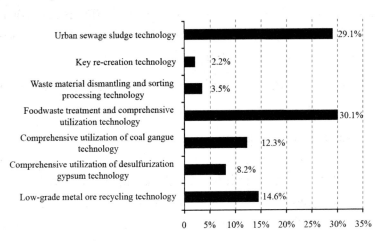

Figure 5 The granted patents distribution of the main fields of the resources recycling industry

5.2 The domestic and foreign granted patents distributions of the resources recycling industry

Figure 6 shows the domestic and foreign granted patents

distributions of major technologies in the resources recycling industry in China. Three features could be drawn from it. Firstly, the number of domestic granted patents is more than that of foreign granted patents in the resources recycling industry in China. Secondly, the granted patents numbers of the food waste treatment and comprehensive utilization industry and the urban sewage sludge recycling industry are the key technical fields at home and abroad, however the granted patents number of the key re-creation technologies is relatively low, especially the number of foreign patents. Thirdly, the domestic granted patents number is accounted for a larger ratio of the comprehensive utilization of coal gangue technology, while the proportion of the foreign granted patents is very low. This indicates that the domestic innovational capability is stronger in the comprehensive utilization of coal gangue technology, and the foreign innovational capability is stronger in the waste material dismantling and sorting processing technology.

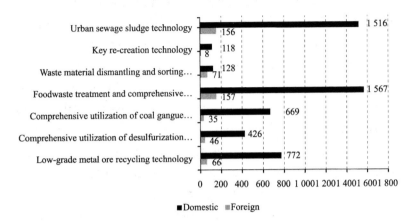

Figure 6 The domestic and foreign granted patents distributions of major fields of the resources recycling industry

We could make a conclusion: the food waste treatment and comprehensive utilization and the urban sewage sludge recycling technologies are the major innovative technical fields at home and abroad in the resources recycling industry; the comprehensive utilization of coal gangue technology place an important role in technical innovations of the resources recycling industry.

6. The Granted Patents Distributions of the Environmental Management Industry

Main technologies of the resource recycling industry include the heavy metal wastewater, waste gas, waste residue pollution control technology (C02F1/62–C02F1/64, B01D53/64), the flue gas desulfurization technology

(B01D53/48-B01D53/60), the high concentration organic wastewater control technology (C02F1/00-C02F1/78, C02F3/00-C02F3/34, C02F9/00-C02F9/14), the heavy metals & POPs (Persistent Organic Pollutants) contaminated soil remediation technology (B09C1/00-B09C1/10).

6.1 The granted patents distribution of main fields of the environmental management industry

From the granted patents distribution of main technologies in the environmental management industry (Figure 7), we could find that the granted patents number of the environmental management industry is 18 270 from 2008 to 2013, which is completely unbalanced to other technical fields. In other words, more than 80% of granted patents in the industry focused on the high concentration organic wastewater control technology. The granted patents number of the high concentration organic wastewater control technology is more than others. There are serious problems of industrial organic waste water stimulated technological innovations in this field. The continuous innovation abilities of the heavy metal wastewater, waste gas, waste residue pollution control technology and the heavy metals & POPs contaminated soil remediation technology are insufficient, accounted for only about 3% of the granted patents number of the industry.

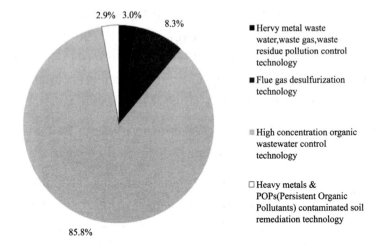

Figure 7 The granted patents distribution of main technologies of the environmental management industry

Therefore, the innovative capability of the high concentration organic wastewater control technology is the strongest, while the innovative capabilities of the heavy metal wastewater, waste gas, waste residue pollution control technology and the heavy metals & POPs contaminated soil remediation technology still need to greatly improve.

6.2 The domestic and foreign granted patents distributions of the environmental management industry

As shown in the granted patents distributions of the environmental management industry at home and abroad (Figure 8), we could find the following features. Firstly, the domestic granted patents number is far more than the foreign granted patents number of the environmental management industry in China. Secondly, the distributions of domestic and foreign granted patents both significantly concentrate on the high concentration organic wastewater control technical field. It indicates that the technical field of the high concentration organic wastewater control technology is the key domain in the environmental management industry in China.

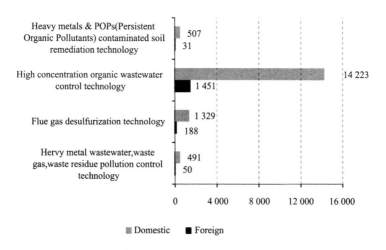

Figure 8 The domestic and foreign granted patents distributions of the environmental management industry

7. Conclusions

The energy-saving and environmental protection industry is one of the seven strategic emerging industries, which is the key industry to change the economic development

mode, promote and upgrade the industrial chain in China.[1]
By analyzing the granted patents distribution of the energy-saving and environmental protection industry in China from 2008 to 2013, we could draw the following four conclusions: Firstly, the technological development of the energy-saving and environmental protection industry developed rapidly, but the development of sub-technology industries is not balanced, and the innovative capability of the environmental management industry is the strongest. Secondly, technological innovations of the energy-saving industry are focused on the environmentally air-conditioning and heat pump technology, and technological innovations of the resources recycling industry are mainly concentrated on the food waste treatment and comprehensive utilization technology and the urban sewage sludge recycling technology, and technological innovations of the environmental management industry are highly focused on the high concentration organic wastewater control technology. Thirdly, the granted patents distributions of the key strategic technical fields are unbalanced, of which the granted patents of the environmental management industry have the largest share. Fourthly, the domestic granted patents distributions are basically similar to that of foreign granted patents in the energy-saving and environmental

---

[1] Zhang Yangping, Tang Xuan. (2012). Development theories of strategic emerging industries and practice experiences for reference: A case study of the energy saving and environmental protection industry in Guangdong province. *Modern Urban Research*, 27(7): 81-87. (in Chinese)

protection industry in China, but the numbers of domestic granted patents are more than the numbers of foreign granted patents.

IV. Research on the Distribution of Patented Technologies of Energy-saving Industry in China[*]

Abstract: The energy-saving industry is an important part of the energy-saving and environmental protection industry, which is one of seven strategic emerging industries in China. By analyzing the distribution of patented technologies of the energy-saving industry in China, the following conclusions can be drawn: the energy-saving industry is not yet mature, with the competition in industrial technology fiercer; the distributions of patented technologies is unbalanced, of which innovation activities in the technological field of the environmentally air-conditioning and heat pump is more active; Japan, Korea and other multinational companies are more prominent in the development of energy-saving industry in China; the domestic technological innovation is dominant in quantity, while some core technologies are still powerful controlled by foreign patentees.

Keywords: Energy-saving, Patented Technologies, Distribution

1. Introduction

Since the 20th century, the growth of the world economy is unprecedented, but along with the economic development,

---

    * Yongzhong Qiao, Qi Liang. Research on the Distribution of Patented Technologies of the Energy-saving Industry in China, Advanced Materials Research, 2014, (1008～1009):1399～1404.

environmental problems have become increasingly prominent. Global warming, resource depletion, biodiversity loss, environmental pollution, desertification and other environmental problems are becoming increasingly threatening the survival of humanity. The issue that how to ensure economic and social development, while not damaging the environment, has gradually become a priority in various countries. Therefore, the environmental protection industry attracts more and more attention in most countries. The energy-saving and environmental protection industry is one of seven strategic emerging industries in China,[1] with granted patents growth rate of 34.94% in 2012, which is higher than that of other granted patents in the corresponding period.[2] Energy-saving industry is one of the sub-industries in energy-saving and environmental protection industry, which is also the key industry for development in the Twelfth Five-Year Development Plan of China. Energy-saving industry has become an important force of China's economic growth in the emerging industry.

China's energy-saving technology develops rapidly, especially after China regarded it as one of key strategic emerging industries. The innovation activities of energy-saving technologies are prosperous, and more and more researches are focusing on the technology development and other relative

---

[1] The State Council of PRC. (2010). *Development plans of "12th five-year" for the national strategic emerging industries.*

[2] State Intellectual Property Office (SIPO). The total reports of patents statistical analysis in strategic emerging industries. in http://www.sipo.gov.cn/tjxx/, 2014-05-13.

issues.[1] Patent is one of the most reliable measures of the most direct indicators of technological innovation,[2] which would reflect the latest trends of researches in the industry and make companies develop their own technological strategies.[3] The patent's quantity and quality have become a key force in the development of energy-saving industry both in China and the world.

Though plenty of results of studies have been carried on, most are still pointing on qualitative analysis from a macro perspective, lacking of quantitative and empirical researches on technology patents. Hence, the theoretical support for the development of energy-saving industry is insufficient. In order to clarify the characteristics of the development of China's energy-saving technology, and to provide a wider field of theoretical support for it, we quantitatively analyze status and trends of the development of patents of China's energy-saving industry related technologies, providing more references.

2. Data Source and Technology Classification

In this article, the patents statistics is searched by IPC

---

[1]   Jianling Zhang, Guoshun Wang. Energy saving technologies and productive efficiency in the Chinese iron and steel sector. *Energy*. 2008,33(4):525-537.

[2]   Janghyeok Y, Kwangsoo K. (2012). An analysis of property-function based patent networks for strategic R&D planning in fast-moving industries: The case of silicon-based thin film solar cells. *Expert Systems with Applications*, 39(9):4409-7717.

[3]   Brent B. A, Walter G. P. (2007). The influence of patent protection on firm innovation investment in manufacturing industries. *Journal of International Management*, 13 (2):91-109.

(International Patent Classification) in the platform of patent-searching system of Patent Star (http://searchtel. patentstar. com.cn/) from 2008 to 2013; and the information of patents of the energy-saving industry is analyzed; then the development trends and patent problems in the industry in China are exposed.

The technical fields of the energy-saving industry includes the industrial boiler design and manufacturing technology, the waste heat and energy utilization technology, and the environmentally air conditioning and heat pump technology. Their main technical areas involved the IPC symbols are based on the *"Patent Search Handbook in Strategic Emerging Industries"*.[1] The IPC codes of the technical fields of energy-saving industry are shown in Table 1.

Table 1 The IPC codes of the technical fields of the energy-saving industry in China

Technical fields	IPC codes
Industrial boiler design and manufacturing technology	F22B9/00-F22B9/18;F22B27/00-F22B27/16; F22B29/00-F22B29/12
Waste heat and energy utilization technology	F27D17/00
Environmentally air conditioning and heat pump technology	F24F1/00-F24F1/04;F24F3/00-F24F3/16;F24F5/00; F25B30/00-F25B30/06

---

[1] Hunan intellectual property bureau, *Patent Search Handbook in Strategic Emerging Industries*. Beijing: Intellectual Property Publishing House, 2012.

3. The Patent Distributions of Main Technologies in the Energy-saving Industry

3.1 Technological innovation characteristics of the energy-saving industry in China

With statistics of nearly six years of granted patents the energy-saving industry in China, we can draw the status and trends of patented technologies in the industry. Fig.1 shows the trend of granted patents the energy-saving industry in China from 2008 to 2013, from which we can get the information on changes of granted-patents technology by years. As shown in Fig.1, the grants of The energy industry in Chinatechnology patents were 3 322, a dramatic promotion compared with the early development of the industry. The grants is not growing year by year, but a form of wavy growth. Though China listed the energy-saving and environmental protection industry as one of strategic emerging industries in 2010, there is no significant improvement in granted patents in the industry. It indicates that the industrial structure of the energy-saving industry in China is not yet mature, with a unstable development. There may be two reasons accounting for that: on the one hand, since China's energy-saving industry started late, and is subject to constraints to the level of industrial technologies, the technological innovation capacity is insufficient;[1] for the other hand, by the simple pursuit of influence GDP over the past years, local governments vigorously develop the extensive industrial economy, lacking of attention to the energy saving, without giving any proper policy support and guidance, and finally, resulting in the lacks of motivation in the field of energy technology innovation.

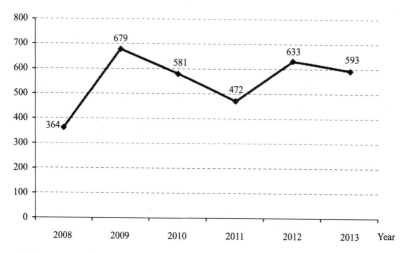

Figrue 1 The development trend of granted patents the energy-saving industry in China (2008 ~ 2013)

---

[1] Liu Shumei, Liu Yuping. Analysis of present situation and proposals for development measures of environmental protection industry in China. *Environmental science and management*, 2005, 30(3):11-12.

3.2 Distributions of grantedpatents in the technological fields of industrial boiler design and manufacturing and waste heat and energy utilization

Table 2 shows that distributions of grantedpatents in the technological fields of industrial boiler design and manufacturing and waste heat and energy utilization from 2008 to 2013. As can be seen from Table 1, innovation activities in the two fields are not active, totally granted 423, accounting for 12.73% of patents of the energy-saving industry. The creative capability of industrial boiler design and manufacturing technology is obviously insufficient, only granted 35 patents in the past 6 years. In specific technical items, the grants of F22B27/00-F22B27/16, only granted 8 patents, are the least, while F27D17/00 gets a relatively large amount.

Compared with foreign patentees, the granted patents of domestic take an absolute advantage both in the two technical fields, with a number of 361, accounting for 85.34% of the total granted patents in the two technological fields. And foreign patentees were granted only 62 patents. It shows that in terms of quantity, there is not threat to the related technology development in China for foreign patentees in the two domains.

Table 2 Distributions of granted patents in the technological fields of industrial boiler design and manufacturing technology and waste heat and energy utilization（2008 ~ 2013）

States/ Areas	Industrial boiler design and manufacturing technology			waste heat and energy utilization technology
	F22B9/00– F22B9/16	F22B27/00– F22B27/16	F22B29/00– F22B29/12	F27D17/00
CN	12	4	6	339
JP	0	0	0	19
KR	0	2	0	0
EU	0	2	9	16
USA	0	0	0	6
OTHERS	0	0	0	8
TOTAL	12	8	15	388
		35		388

F22B9/00-F22B9/16：Steam boilers of fire-tube type, i.e. the flue gas from a combustion chamber outside the boiler body flowing through tubes built–in in the boiler body；F22B27/00-F22B27/16：Instantaneous or flash steam boilers；F22B29/00-F22B29/12：Steam boilers of forced-flow type；F27D17/00：Arrangement for using waste heat (heat-exchangers per seF28); Arrangement for using, or disposing of, waste gases (removing fumes in general B08B 15/00).

3.3 Distributions of granted patents in the technological fields of environmentally air conditioning and heat pump

Table 3 shows distributions of grantedpatents in the technological fields of environmentally air conditioning and heat pump technology. As shown in table 3, the innovative capabilities in the field of environmentally air conditioning and heat pump technology are strongest the energy-saving industry in China. The granted patents occupy the absolute advantage in the industry, with a total of 2,899 patents, accounting for 87.27% of total patents. In specific technical items, four specific technologies in the field develop well, of which granted patents are higher than other areas of specific technical items. The amount of F24F1/00-F24F1/04 technology item is the most, up to 1025 granted patents.

Compared with foreign patentees, 1808 patents are granted to the domestic patentees, while the foreign patentees get 1092. It can be seen that the competition between domestic and abroad is fierce, and the development of domestic technology is not dominant in the field of environmentally air conditioning and heat pump technology. Foreign patentees are most from Japan, Korea, the European Union and the United States and other countries or regions. Japan and South Korea patentees attain a larger grants among the foreign patentees, accounting for 87% of the total foreign giants.

The energy-saving industry in China, the key researches, domestic and abroad, are consistent, both absolutely focusing on the field of environmentally air conditioning and heat pump technology. Although the domestic granted patents take advantage in the overall numerical value, domestic granted patents are lower than other countries in some specific technical items. For instance, in the technical item of F24F1/00-F24F1/04, the domestic shared 462 patents, while foreign patentees get 563 patents granted, 101 more than the domestic. It indicates that some core technologies are still controlled by foreign patentees in China's energy-saving industry, hindering the further development of domestic industry.

Table 3 Distributions of granted patents in the technological field of environmentally air conditioning and heat pump (2008 ~ 2013)

States/ Areas	Environmentally air conditioning and heat pump technology			
	F24F1/00-F24F1/04	F24F3/00-F24F3/16	F24F5/00	F25B30/00-F25B30/06
CN	462	532	447	367
JP	295	163	77	34
KR	257	89	19	15
EU	7	37	15	6
USA	2	31	7	9
OTHERS	2	14	6	6
TOTAL	1025	866	571	437
	2899			

F24F1/00-1/04:Room units, e.g. separate or self-contained units or units receiving primary air from a central station ; F24F3/00-3/16:Air-conditioning systems in which conditioned primary air is supplied from one or more central stations to distributing units in the rooms or spaces where it may receive secondary treatment; Apparatus specially designed for such systems; F24F5/00: Air-conditioning systems or apparatus not covered by group F24F 1/00 or F24F 3/00; F25B30/00-30/06: Heat pumps.

4. Conclusions

The energy-saving and environmental protection industry is one of the seven strategic emerging industries, which is the key industry to change the economic development mode, promote and upgrade the industrial chain in China.[1] As an important part of energy-saving and environmental protection industry, the development of energy-saving industry will greatly promote the development of energy-saving and environmental protection industry in China. The patent system may improve the green technological innovation capability through a continuous cycle process: technological exploitation – protection – utilization – improvement – protection – utilization.[2]

By analyzing the patents distribution of the energy-saving industry in China from 2008 to 2013, we could draw the following four conclusions: First, at present, the development of energy-saving industry in China is not yet mature, with a wave patent growth by years. Second, the development of various technologies the energy-saving industry in China is uneven, mainly concentrated on the field of environmentally air conditioning and heat pump technology. And in technology-specific items, granted patents are more focusing on F24F1/00-F24F1/04. Third, the amount of domestic patents is dominant in the overall numerical value, but some core technologies are still controlled by foreign technology patent powers like Japan, South Korea, America and

[1] Zhang Yangping, Tang Xuan. Development theories of strategic emerging industries and practice experiences for reference: A case study of the energy saving and environmental protection industry in Guangdong province. *Modern Urban Research*, 2012, 27(7): 81-87.

[2] Liu Fudong, Zhu Xuezhong, Wen Jiachun. Study on the patent system oriented to low-carbon develop. *China Soft Science Magazine*, 2011, (7): 25-30.

European Union. Fourth, the key researches, domestic and abroad, are consistent in the energy-saving industry in China, as well as the patent distributions in different technological fields.

V. Research on the Granted Patent Distributions of Significance Firms in the New Energy Automobile Industry in China[*]

Abstract: By analyzing the granted patent distributions of key technical fields on the representative automobile firms Chery, BYD, Geely and Changan in China from 2008 to 2013, conclusions can be drawn as follows: In the hybrid power field, there is no big difference among the technological innovation achievements, and the overall granted patents are of high quality; In the blade electric vehicles field, there is a balanced development, and less the extreme phenomenon in the amount of granted patents, simultaneously it enjoys an obvious advantage; In the fuel cell vehicle field, the amount of granted patents is relatively low, and the extreme phenomenon and the unbalanced distribution of granted patents are obvious; In the battery technical field, the amount of granted patents is high, but still there exists significant gaps among the granted patent distributions of enterprises.

Keywords: New energy; Automobile; Patent; Distribution

1. Introduction

The new energy vehicles is a new technology and new structure car, which adopts an unconventional vehicle fuel

---

* Yongzhong Qiao, Tiantian Zhang. Research on the Granted Patent Distributions of Significance Firms in the New Energy Automobile Industry in China. 2014 Global Conference on Environmental Engineering (GCEE2014).

such as the power source or the conventional vehicle fuels, and which adopts some advanced technologies such as the new-vehicle power unit, the dynamics control vehicle etc. The new energy automotive industry, which is engaged in the production and the use of new energy automotive industry, is one of seven strategic emerging industries in China. It is very important to study on the granted patents distributions of this technical field for the technological innovation and development of the new energy automotive industry.

Comparative analysis on the patent distributions of technical fields in representative firms can provide important reference for the development of related industries in China.[1] Existing studies mainly focus on the new energy industry policies, the overall analysis of the development strategy in the new energy automotive industry. As studies have shown, the United States will mainly focus on the hydrogen-powered fuel cell vehicles, and the hybrid cars will be developed by Japan in feature.[2] The biggest problems restricting the development of the new energy automotive industry in China are the high expenditure, the low capacity and the instability of battery.[3] There is the inadequate of technological innovation ability, the shortage

[1] Luan Chunjuan, Wang Xukun, Liu Zeyuan. Comparative study on the patents distributions of Samsung electronics Co., Ltd. and Huawei technologies Co., Ltd., *Scientific Management Research*. 2(2008):117-121. (in Chinese)

[2] Yanghaixia. The opportunities of the new energy vehicles in China, *China Investment*. 9(2008):11. (in Chinese)

[3] Yuan Huazhi, Jian Xiaoping, Yuan Huajian. Research on the competitiveness of the new energy vehicle industry in China, *Science and Technology Management Research*, 17(2012):42. (in Chinese)

of infrastructure in the development of new energy vehicles. [1] So China must bypass these technical barriers, and enhance the level of technological innovation, and promote the development of new energy vehicles, at same time upgrades the traditional automotive technology.[2] The research results of the new energy research industry mainly focus on the following aspects: statistical analysis of the patents types, the application subjects and the key technical fields in new energy vehicles;[3] comparative analysis of patents in the new energy automobile industry in China and Japan;[4] the patent standardization of the new energy automobile industry in China;[5] the patent distributions of brand cars in the new energy technology;[6] comparative study of patent situation of key technologies in the new energy vehicles in China,

[1] Chen Liuqin. Problems and challenges of the new energy vehicle industry in China, *Electricity*, 2(2012):6–9.

[2] Li Wenhui, Sun Chenguang. The possibility and the path selection to achieve the leap development of the new energy automobile, *Chinese Business*, 12(2012):372–373. (in Chinese)

[3] Xu Guoxiang, Yu Bitao, Li Fushen, Ai Juan. The analysis of patent application for the new energy automobile in China, *The Battery*, 5(2012):289–292. (in Chinese)

[4] Zheng Wei. Research on the technology patent of the new energy vehicles, *Automotive Engineering*, 5(2009):43–45. (in Chinese)

[5] Li Werwer. The Strategy formulation and implementation of the patent standardization in the new energy automotive industry *China Scrence and Technology Forum*, 6(2012):62-68. (in Chinese)

[6] Wang Yong, Wang Zhanglin. The patent analysis of the new energy technology in independent brand automotive enterprises, *Automotive Engineers*, 4(2012):19–21. (in Chinese)

Japan and the United States and other developed countries.[1]
In addition, Guangdong Province in China has released "the
patent analysis and forewarning reports on the new energy
automotive industry", [2] Changzhou of Jiangsu Province in
China has issued "the patent forewarning analysis on the new
energy vehicle industry".[3] Key enterprises are backbones of
the industrial development, but the patent distributions and
trends of key technologies of major enterprises in the new
energy vehicles has been a little reported.

This paper intends to take Chery Automobile Co., Ltd.
(referred to as "Chery"), BYD Company Limited (referred
to as "BYD"), Geely Holding Group Co., Ltd. (referred to
as "Geely") and Chang'an automobile Co., Ltd. (referred to
as "Chang'an") for example in the new energy automobile
industry in China, combining with the enterprise development
strategies of the new energy automotive industry, analyze the
patent distribution characteristics and problems of the new
energy automotive industry, provide a theoretical reference
for the development and investment of the new energy
automotive industry.

---

[1] The planning and development division of state intellectual property office in
China. *Situational analysis report on the patents of the new energy automobile industry.*
11(2012):1-16. (in Chinese)

[2] The patent analysis and early warning report of strategic emerging industries -
new energy automotive industry in Guangdong Province in China, http://www.gdipo.gov.cn/
shared/news_content.aspx?news_id=9161. 2013-12-2. (in Chinese)

[3] The early warning analysis report on the patent of new energy vehicle industry
in Jiangsu changzhou in China, http://www.chinairn.com/news/20130330/114543203.html.
2013-12-2. (in Chinese)

2. Technical Fields and Data Retrieval

2.1 Technical fields

The new energy vehicles includes the hybrid electric vehicles (HEV), the blade electric vehicles (BEV, including solar power car), the fuel cell electric vehicle (FCEV), the hydrogen engine vehicles, and other new energy sources (such as the high energy storage devices, DME) cars and other categories of products. The developing direction of the technological innovation mainly focuses on the hybrid vehicles, the blade electric vehicles and the fuel cell vehicles.

2.2 Key Enterprises

On the domestic patent applications, the first three enterprises are Chery, BYD and Chang'an in the hybrid vehicles field; the first three enterprises are BYD, Chery, Tsinghua University in the blade electric vehicles field; the first two enterprises are Tsinghua University, Shanghai God in the fuel cell vehicle field; the top three enterprises are BYD, Chery, Tianjin Power of God in the battery technical field. Therefore, this article focuses on the distribution characteristics and problems of granted patents of the Chery, BYD, Geely and Chang'an in China.

2.3 Data Retrieval

All patent data in this article are searched from the SooPat patent database (http://www2.soopat.com/Home/IIndex), retrieval method is "apply subjects + IPC classification codes", the interval time from 2008 to 2013, and then statistics the information of granted patents of four enterprises. In additional, the individual IPC codes of different technical fields may be repeated, so some statistics data taken by labor.

3. Data Analysis

3.1 The Overall Distributions of Granted Patents of Four Technological Fields

The distribution of granted patents in the hybrid vehicles field, the blade electric vehicles field, the fuel cell vehicles field and the battery technical fields in Chery, BYD, Geely and Chang'an from 2008 to2013 shows as Figure 1.

As can be seen from Figure 1, in the hybrid cars fields, the differences of granted patent number of Chery, BYD, and Geely are small, but the granted patent number of Changan is significantly disadvantage. In the blade electric vehicles field, the polarization of granted patents number is not obvious. In the fuel cell vehicles field, the numbers of granted patents of Chery, Geely and Chang'an are relatively low, only a few granted patents. In the battery technical field, the advantage of granted patents of four enterprises are obvious, especially BYD' total reached 732, which is more than the sum of the other three enterprises.

Specifically, the characteristics of granted patents distribution in four key technical fields in four enterprises as following: firstly, BYD's granted patents number is the largest in four technical fields, and it obtained an absolute advantage in the battery technical fields; secondly, Chang'an's granted patents number behind other three companies in the hybrid cars field, which indicates that its technology innovation level is relatively backward in the field; thirdly, Geely's granted patents number of the blade electric vehicles field is less than that of the hybrid vehicles field, and the focal point of patent distribution are vary in the different fields; fourthly, from the total number of granted patents, Chang'an's overall number of granted patents is relatively low, although the granted patents number of the battery technical field is higher than other technical fields.

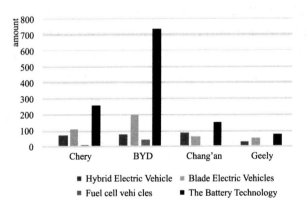

Figure 1 The overall distributions of granted patents
of four technical fields

3.2 Distributions of Granted Patents in the Hybrid Electric Vehicle Field

The hybrid car is a generators car, which equipped with two or more power sources, such as batteries, fuel cells, solar cells or locomotives. In the transition process of from a traditional car to a new energy car, the hybrid power is the only way for the technological development of enterprises. The distribution of granted patents of the hybrid vehicle technical field in four companies shows as Table 1.

Table 1 The distributions of granted patents in the hybrid electric vehicle field

	Chery	BYD	Geely	Chang'an
The arrangement or installation of prime mover (B60K6)[1]	13+0[2]	37+16	34+18	5+2
The vehicle control system (B60W20)	15+0	6+1	4+3	8+0
The power electric traction (B60L11)	13+1	4+6	8+4	3+0
The joint control of vehicle subsystems (B60W10)	24+2	8+0	7+5	8+2
Total	68	78	83	28

---

[1] The International Patent Classification represents the whole body of knowledge which may be regarded as proper to the field of patents for invention, divided into eight sections. Sections are the highest level of hierarchy of the classification.

[2] The data format: invention patents + utility model patents.

Seen from Table1, there are the following characteristics of the hybrid vehicle technical fields in four firms. Firstly, in the arrangement or installation of prime mover technical field, BYD and Geely's granted patents have an advantage, the Chang'an's and Chery granted patents numbers are relatively lower; In the vehicle control system field, Chery's granted patents number is of an obvious advantage, and BYD, Chang'an's and Geely granted patent numbers are a few; In power electric traction technical field, Changan's granted patents are fewer; In the joint control of the vehicle subsystems technical field, Chery's granted patents number is the sum of other three firms, and BYD's granted patents are few. Secondly, in Chery, the granted patent number is more balance in various technical fields, and it has an obvious advantages in the joint control of vehicle subsystems technical field; In the arrangement or installation of prime mover field, BYD and Geely have an absolute advantage, and its granted patent number is more than the total number of granted patents of other technical fields in this firm; In Chang'an, the amount of granted patents is relatively small, and there are only a few granted patents in the major technical fields. Finally, in the hybrid cars field, the number of granted invention patents in various technical fields is much higher than the amount of granted utility model patents, indicating all enterprises focuses on the technological innovation and the quality of granted patents.

It can clearly be seen that the total of granted patents of Chery, BYD and Geely are little difference, but Chang'an's granted patents number is fewer in the hybrid vehicles field. In this technical field, the ratio of granted invention patents is high; and the ratio of utility model patents is relatively low in four enterprises.

3.3 Distributions of Granted Patents in the Blade Electric Vehicle Field

The granted patents distributions of the blade electric vehicle technical field in four enterprises in 2008 ~ 2013 as shown in Table 2. According to Table 2, in the blade electric vehicles field, BYD's granted patents number is the largest, Chery's granted patents number is second, and their competitive advantage are obvious; Changan's and Geely granted patents numbers are closer, and the total is small.

According to Table 2, four distribution characteristics of granted patents can be found in four major technical fields in four companies. Firstly, in the power electric traction technical field, Chery's granted patent number is relatively large, BYD and Geely have only two patents, Changan has not granted patent in this field. Combining with the content of Table 1, we can discovery that the power electric traction technical field not only involves the blade electric vehicle technology, but also belong to the core technology of the hybrid vehicles field and the fuel cell vehicles field. This indicates that there is a certain the cross and contact among the technical fields in the new energy automotive industry. Secondly, in the battery pack/power supply technical field, granted patents technologies most concentrated in four enterprises, of which BYD's advantages is particularly obvious, and the number of granted patents reached 137, but more than 60% of the number is utility model patents. Thirdly, in the battery and manufacturing technical field and the arrangement/installation of vehicle drive fields, the granted patents distributions of four firms are relatively uniform, and BYD has a little advantage. It is worth noting that Chang'an has relatively strong competitiveness in the three technical fields. Finally, Chery's invention patents amount is much higher than the amount of utility model patents, however, BYD, Geely and Chang'an's proportions of utility model patents are higher, which indicates Chery pay more attention to improve its patent quality.

Table 2 The distributions of granted patents in the blade electric vehicle field

	Chery	BYD	Geely	Chang'an
The power electric traction（B60L11）	13+3	0+2	2+0	0
The battery pack/power supply（H02J7）	44+14	57+80	12+20	11+3
The battery and manufacturing（H01M10）	8+0	10+16	2+5	6+4
The manufacturing method and structural components（H01M2）	4+3	4+6	0+9	4+10
The vehicle drive arrangement/installation（B60K17）	8+7	4+15	0+7	3+9
Total	104	194	57	50

In short, in the blade electric vehicles field, the development trends of four enterprises are relatively balance, and the overall advantage of this field is more prominent, the extreme phenomenon of granted patents is not obvious. BYD is a leader of granted patents, but Chery has greater invention patents, which more focus on the patent quality.

3.4 Distributions of Granted Patents in the Fuel Cell Electric Vehicle Field

Since the fuel cell electric vehicle can achieve the zero emissions of carbon dioxide, and it has the long mileage, the short fueling time and other advantages, it is an ultimate direction of the automotive development in future. But the technological innovation of the fuel cell vehicles field is not obvious. The granted patents distributions of the fuel cell electric vehicle field four firms as shown in Table 3. According to Table 3, BYD's number of granted patents is the largest, followed by Chery, and Geely and Chang'an's number of granted patents are rare. It shows that there is serious technical level differentiation in this field in four firms. This paper argues that there are two reasons for this phenomenon: Firstly, BYD's predecessor is a battery manufacturer, which has the first granted patent battery technology, so it has an absolute advantage in the electric vehicles field in China; Secondly, BYD had established the Academia Sinica, the Electronic Research Institute of Automotive, the Engineering Research Institute and the Electric Power Research Institute, which are responsible for the development of high-tech products and technologies in this technical field.

Table 3 The distributions of granted patents in the fuel cell electric vehicle field

	Chery	BYD	Geely	Chang'an
The fuel cell and manufacturing (H01M8)	0	17+4	2+0	1+0
The electrode elements (H01M4)	1+0	0	0	0
The power electric traction (B60L11)	0	0	0	0
The input into output of DC power (H02M3)	8+3	12+11	0	0+1
Total	14	44	2	3

The distribution characteristics of granted patents in the fuel cell vehicle technical field in four firms showed the following aspects. Firstly, the granted patents of the electrode elements field and the power electric traction technical field almost are zero. The electrode elements technology involves more the lithium iron phosphate sub-cell, and it's not much correlation with the fuel cell. The power electric traction technology is the core technology of the hybrid vehicles and the blade electric vehicles. There is not a patent in the power electric traction field in four firms. Secondly, in the fuel cell vehicle technical field, the granted patents mainly focus on the fuel cell and manufacturing field and the input into output of DC power technical fields.

We can clearly see that the overall amount of granted patents is lower, in the last one of four technical fields in the fuel cell vehicles field. And in this field, the distribution granted patents is not uniform, and the extreme phenomenon is obvious, and the technological innovation needs to further strengthen.

3.5 Distributions of Granted Patents in the battery technical Field

From the distributions of granted patents in the battery technical field in four enterprises (Table 4) can find that four firms all are more concerned on the granted patent distributions of the battery technical field, and the proportion of granted patents number in this field accounted for the total of granted patents number is higher. Because that electricity replace oil is the key of that the new energy vehicles replace the fuel powered automobile. Therefore, whether the hybrid vehicles, the blade electric vehicles, or the fuel cell vehicles, all belong to the new energy vehicles, which use electricity as the primary power source. So the battery technology will be inevitably become the core technology of research and development of various enterprises.

According to Table 4, in the field of battery technology, BYD's granted patents number is far beyond the sum of other three firms. There are obvious advantages for the granted patents distribution of the battery and manufacturing field, the manufacturing methods of structural components field and the electrode elements field. The proportion of invention patents to utility model patents in the battery and manufacturing field is basically flat. The proportion of utility model patents in the manufacturing methods of structural components field is relatively higher. In the electrode elements field, the amount of granted invention patents is majority. These facts indicate that the distribution of granted patent types is difference in different technical fields. In the circuits or fluid lines and original layout field and the arrangement or installation of electric power plant field, BYD's granted patents number is relatively low and the types of patents mainly is utility model patents. This indicates that BYD has not advantage in these technical fields.

Table 4 The distributions of granted patents in the battery technical field

	Chery	BYD	Geely	Chang'an
The battery and manufacturing (H01M10)	43+4	142+108	1+7	7+6
The manufacturing method of structural components (H01M2)	21+12	72+133	0+5	6+3
The electrode elements (H01M4)	61+1	205+15	0	0
The circuits or fluid lines and original layout (B60R16)	61+24	5+25	30+82	12+29
The arrangement or installation of electric power plant (B60K1)	15+16	3+24	4+18	4+13
Total	258	732	147	80

In the battery technical field, Chery's distribution of granted patents is evenly in various key technical fields. Although the granted patents numbers of the manufacturing methods of structural components field and the arrangement and layout of electric power plant field are relatively low, but the gap is small, and the invention patents number is larger. Geely and Chang'an's granted patents number in this field is lower, and the distribution of granted patents has obvious characteristics. First, the granted patents number of the cell and manufacturing field and the manufacturing methods of structural components field are a few, and the granted patents number of the electrode elements field is zero; Second, the granted patents number of the manufacturing methods of structural components field and the arrangement and layout of electric power plant field is relatively high, however, which are mainly the utility model patents, and the patents quality is not high.

This shows that the granted patents numbers of the battery technical field in four enterprises are higher. This field is the key field of patents distribution, however, there are different focuses for the granted patents distribution in the different enterprises, and there are larger gap.

4. Conclusion

By analysis on the granted patents distribution of four key technical fields of Chery, BYD, Geely and Chang'an in new energy automotive industry in China, conclusion can be drawn that, in hybrid field, Chery, BYD, Geely's granted patents number are little difference, and the patent quality is higher, however, Chang'an's granted patents level is lower. In the blade electric vehicles field, the development trends of granted patents are relatively balance, and the overall advantage is obvious, the extreme disparity of granted patents is not obvious, and BYD lie in a leadership position in four enterprises, however, Chery's patents quality is higher. In the fuel cell vehicles field, the total of granted patents is lower, and the distribution of granted patents is uneven, and the extreme phenomenon is obvious. In the battery technical field, the total of granted patents is higher, which is the key field of patent distribution, however, there are obviously gap in four enterprises.

《知识产权专题研究书系》书目